1000 of the World's Funniest Jokes FOR KIDS!

First published in Great Britain in 2002 by
Dean, an imprint of Egmont Books Limited,
239 Kensington High Street,
London W8 6SA

ISBN 0 603 56066 0

1 3 5 7 9 10 8 6 4 2

Printed and bound in the U.A.E.

1000 of the World's Funniest Jokes FOR KIDS!

Written and Compiled by: Guy Campbell & Mark Devins
Illustrated by: Paul Moran & Simon Ecob

What's rich and goes "putt putt putt"?
Tiger Woods!

How do crazy people go through the forest?
They take the psycho-path!

What do prisoners use to call each other?
Cell phones!

What's blond and terrorises cricketers?
Buffy the Umpire Slayer!

How do you shoot a blue elephant?
With a blue elephant gun, of course.

How do you shoot a red elephant?
No, not with a red elephant gun. You strangle him until he turns blue, and then shoot him with a blue elephant gun.

How do you shoot a green elephant?
Say something rude so he goes red, strangle him until he turns blue, and then shoot him with a blue elephant gun.

How do you shoot a yellow elephant?
Have you ever seen a yellow elephant?

How do you get hold of seaweed?
Put a sign up saying "Kelp Wanted"!

A man at a swimming pool was on the very top diving board. He posed, lifted his arms, and was about to dive when the attendant came running up, shouting, "Don't dive! There's no water in the pool!"
"That's all right," said the man. "I can't swim!"

"A pound of kidleys please, Butcher!"
"You mean a pound of kidneys."
"That's what I said, diddle I?"

A lady gets on the bus. "Does this bus stop at the village pond?" she asks the driver.
"I hope so," he says, "I can't swim!"

What do you call a madman on a mountain bike?
A Cyclepath!

Boy: Mom, why can't I swim in Loch Ness?
Mother: Because there are monsters in it.
Boy: But Daddy's swimming there.
Mother: That's different. He's insured!

Did you hear about the sword swallower who swallowed an umbrella?
He wanted to put something away for a rainy day!

Fred: Do you think that women talk more than men?
Harry: No, they just use more words!

Patient: Doctor, every time I drink a cup of tea I get a sharp stabbing pain in my eye!
Doctor: Have you tried taking the spoon out of the cup?

Who is in films and always broke?
Skint Eastwood!

Who makes suits and eats spinach?
Popeye the Tailorman!

Patient: Tell me honestly, how am I?
Dentist: Your teeth are fine, but your gums will have to come out!

What always starts with a tie?
A three-legged race!

George: Dad, would you like to save some money?
Dad: I certainly would, son. Any suggestions?
George: Yes. Why not buy me a bike, then I won't wear my shoes out so fast!

What do you call a man with a wooden head?
Edward!

What do you call a man with three wooden heads?
Edward Woodward!

What do you call a monster with four wooden heads?
I don't know but Edward Woodward would!

Frog 1: What is that son of yours doing these days?
Frog 2: He's at medical school.
Frog 1: Oh, what's he studying?
Frog 2: Nothing, they're studying him!

What do bulls do when they go shopping?
They CHARGE!

A Scotsman is paying his first visit to the zoo, and he stops by one of the cages. "An' whut animal would that be?" he asked the nearby keeper.
"That's a moose from Canada," the keeper replies.
"A moose!" exclaimed the Scotsman.
"Och, they must ha' rats like rhinos over there!"

What do you get if you cross a pig and an emergency vehicle?
A Hambulance!

What do you get if you cross a joke book and a snowstorm?
Corn Flakes!

What do you get if you cross a pig and a telephone?
A lot of crackling on the line!

What do you get if you cross a vampire and a plumber?
A drain in the neck!

What do you get if you cross a vampire and a mummy?
Something you wouldn't want to unwrap!

There was a tremendous racket on the staircase. Johnny ran out to find his grandad at the bottom of the stairs in a heap.
"Blimey, Grandad, did you miss a step?" said Johnny.
"No, I think I caught them all!"

What do you get if you cross a bike and a rose?
Bicycle petals!

What do we get from naughty cows?
Bad milk!

Did you hear about the monster who had twelve arms and no legs?
He was all fingers and thumbs!

Customer: Waiter, how long have you worked here?
Waiter: Six months, sir.
Customer: Well, it can't have been you who took my order, then!

Waiter, waiter! There's a mosquito in my soup.
Don't worry sir, they don't eat much!

"Why aren't you eating your stew, Bobby?" said Granny. "Because it's really tough, Gran!" said Bobby. Granny takes a forkful of stew. "Oh honestly!" she says, "It's not that tough!" "It isn't now," said Bobby,
"I've been chewing it for twenty minutes."

What did the teddy bear say to the waiter when he offered him some pudding?
No thanks. I'm stuffed!

How do you catch a squirrel?
Climb a tree and act like a nut!

What do you give a dog with a fever?
Mustard, it's the best thing for a hot dog!

Patient: Doctor, my sisters think I'm mad because I like peas.
Doctor: There's nothing wrong with that, I like peas, too.
Patient: Oh, good! Come back to my house and I'll show you my collection!

A cowboy had been in the saloon for a while and decided that it was time, once again, to head for the hills. He walked through the swing doors and immediately noticed that his horse had disappeared from the rail. "OK," he said, re-entering the crowded bar, "I'm gonna have one more drink and if my horse ain't back by then, the same thing will happen here that happened in Dodge City."
With that, several of the cowboys ran out of the saloon and within minutes one had returned to tell him that they'd found his horse for him. As he turned to leave, the bar-tender stopped him.
"Excuse me stranger," he said, "but what happened in Dodge City?"
The cowboy replied: "I had to walk home!"

What do you get if you cross a Spice Girl with a pudding?
A Jelly Baby!

What do you get if you cross a skunk with a boomerang?
A horrendous smell that keeps coming back!

A man goes to a restaurant for dinner but he doesn't like the food.
Man: Send the chef here. I wish to complain about this disgusting meal!
Waiter: I'm afraid you'll have to wait, sir. He's just popped out for his dinner.

Two fishermen are out sailing when suddenly a hand appears in the sea. "What's this?" asked the first fisherman. "It looks as if someone is drowning!"
"No," explained the second fisherman, "it's just a little wave!"

What kind of shoes do spies wear?
Sneakers!

What did one wall say to the other wall?
I'll meet you at the corner!

Why is a baseball team like fish and chips?
They both need a decent batter!

Why did the traffic light turn red?
You would too, if you had to change in the middle of the street!

What did one lift say to the other lift?
I think I'm coming down with something!

A little girl is wandering around the beach, crying: "I'm lost, I can't find my Mummy!" A family tries to calm her down; they buy her a hot dog, some sweets and crisps. Soon, a woman comes along and says, "I know where your Mummy is." The girl looks at her and whispers:
"So do I. Now shut up and go away."

What do you get if you cross a telephone and a marriage bureau?
A wedding ring!

Where does Tarzan buy his clothes?
At a Jungle Sale!

Old Harry retired from his job after 50 years and was given a set of golf clubs by his co-workers. Thinking he'd try the game, he asked the local golf professional for some lessons, explaining that he knew nothing whatever about the game. The pro showed him how to stand and swing the club, then said, "Just hit the ball toward the flag on the first green." Harry teed up and smacked the ball straight down the fairway 300 yards and onto the green, where it stopped one inch from the hole. "Now what?" Harry asked the speechless pro.
"Um... you're supposed to hit the ball into the hole," the pro finally said, after he was able to speak again.
"You idiot," said Harry, "why didn't you tell me that before?"

Why did the Romans build straight roads?
So their soldiers didn't go around the bend!

What's a vampire's favourite soup?
Scream of tomato!

A little boy was learning to play the violin. "I'm good, aren't I?" he asked his big brother.
"You should be on the radio," said the brother.
"Wow! Do you you think I'm that good?" said the boy.
"No, but at least if you were on the radio, I could switch you off!"

Patient: Doctor, I think I've been bitten by a vampire!
Doctor: Drink this glass of water.
Patient: Will it make me better?
Doctor: No, but I'll be able to see if your neck leaks!

A man went to see the doctor because he kept bumping into things. "You need glasses," said the doctor, giving him a pair. "Will I be able to read with these?" asked the man. "Yes," said the Doc.
"That's brilliant," said the man. "I couldn't before!"

Did you hear about the man who tried to cross a lion with a goat?
He had to get a new goat!

"I play golf in the low 80's," the little old man was telling one of the young boys at the club.
"Wow," said the young man, "that's pretty impressive."
"Not really," said the little old man.
"If it's any hotter than that I'd probably have a heart attack!"

When can't you bury people who live opposite a graveyard?
When they're not dead!

What is the difference between bogies & broccoli?
Kids won't eat broccoli!

What do you call a Scottish dentist?
Phil McCavity!

How do you get a baby astronaut to sleep?
Rocket!

"I've got a chicken that lays square eggs," said the farmer.
"Really, that's amazing," his friend said.
"Yep, and not only that, it talks as well!" said the farmer.
"No! What does it say?" said his mate.
"It says 'OUCH!'"

Doctor I feel like a pair of curtains...
Pull yourself together!

Did you hear about the man who planted a pen knife in his potato patch?
He was trying to grow chips!

Bobby was a very good little boy. Whenever he was especially good, his Dad would give him ten pence and a pat on the head.
By the time he was sixteen he had £200 and a flat head!

What's yellow and goes slam-slam-slam-slam?
A four-door banana!

What's black and white and bouncy?
A rubber nun!

Why are elephants wrinkly?
Because they hate being ironed!

What happened to the plastic surgeon that stood by the fire?
He melted!

Who sailed the seven seas picking up rubbish?
Binbag the Whaler!

What do you do if a baker faints?
Give him the quiche of life!

The cannibal priest told his flock to close their eyes and say grace.
"For whoever we are about to eat, may the Lord make us truly thankful."

Father: How did the greenhouse get smashed?
Bobby: I was cleaning my catapault and it went off!

What did the alien say to the garden?
Take me to your weeder!

"Why have you stopped playing cards with my sister?"
"Well, would you play with someone who cheats all the time, is a poor loser and keeps tearing up the cards?"
"No, I wouldn't!"
"No, she won't either!"

What musical instrument goes with cheese?
A Picklelo!

Why was 6 afraid of 7?
Because 789!

After a visit to the circus, Geoff and Don were discussing the thrills and marvels they had seen. "I didn't think much of the knife thrower, did you?" said Geoff. "I thought he was great!" enthused Don. "Well, I didn't," said Geoff.
"He kept throwing those knives at that girl but he didn't hit her once!"

Did you hear about the farmer's boy who hated the country? He went to the big city and got a job as a shoe-shine boy.
So the farmer made hay while the son shone!

Sean: Tim's gone to live in the city.
Harry: Why's that?
Sean: He'd read in the papers that the country was at war!

How do you make a Swiss Roll?
Chuck him off an Alp!

Kylie Minogue hires a new assistant called Brian. After about a week she calls him aside for a word. "Brian, you're doing a great job, but you have to remember to knock before you enter my bedroom or bathroom, OK?"
"Don't worry, Miss Minogue," Brian says,
"I always look through the keyhole first, and if you're naked, I don't come in!"

What did the cannibal say when he was full up?
I couldn't eat another mortal!

Doctor: This is a most unusual complaint, Mrs Tibbings. Have you had it before?
Mrs Tibbings: Yes, I have.
Doctor: Well you've got it again!

An Irishman and an American were sitting in the bar at Dublin Airport.
"I've come to meet my brother," said the Irishman. "He's flying in from America in an hour. His first trip home in forty years."
"Will you be able to recognise him?" asked the American.
"I'm sure I won't," said the Irishman, "after all, he's been away for a long time."
"I wonder if he'll recognise you?" said the American.
"Of course he will," said the Irishman. "I haven't been anywhere!"

Doctor, I have an awful lot of wind, can you give me anything for it?
Yes, you can borrow my kite!

Two prisoners escaped from their cells today. One is seven feet tall and the other is four feet six inches tall.
The authorities are looking high and low for them!

Waiter, how long will my pizza be?
We don't do long ones, Sir, only round ones.

What did the cannibal say when he came home and found his wife chopping up a python and a pygmy?
Not snake and pygmy pie again!

Why did the man eat a lava lamp?
He fancied a light snack!

Who was the first underwater spy?
James Pond!

Did you hear about the wooden car with a wooden engine and wooden wheels?
It wooden go!

What do you call a newt from Sydney?
The Lizard of Oz!

What's the difference between an American student and an English student?
About 3,000 miles!

Bill: Hey Phil, are you going fishing?
Phil: Yeah!
Bill: Ya got worms?
Phil: Yeah, but I'm still going!

Bob: This morning I felt that today was going to be my lucky day. I got up at seven, had seven dollars in my pocket, there were seven of us at lunch and there were seven horses in the seven o'clock race - so I bet on number seven.
Terry: Did it work?
Bob: Sort of. It came seventh!

What did one magician say to another?
Who was that girl I sawed you with last night?

Why do traffic wardens have yellow stripes on their hats?
To stop people parking on their faces!

Gaz was having supper with his Gran. "Would you like a cookie?" she asked. "Yes, please," replied Gaz. "What good manners you have!" said Gran. "I do like to hear young people say 'please' and 'thank you'."
"I'll say them both if I can have a big slice of that cake," replied Gaz.

How can you tell which end of a worm is which?
Tickle it in the middle and see which end laughs!

What's small, bright, spotty and has a horn on the end of its nose?
An itsy bitsy teeny weeny yellow polka dot rhinoceros!

A blind rabbit and a blind goat ran into each other in the forest one day. The goat reached out a hoof, touched the rabbit and said, "You're soft and fuzzy and have floppy ears. You must be a rabbit." "You're right!" said the rabbit. Then rabbit reached out, touched the goat and said,
"You've got a wet nose and a beard... You must be a geography teacher!"

What do you call a mayfly with a machine-gun?
Baddy-long-legs!

Why did the robber take a bath?
Because he wanted to make a clean getaway!

A man takes his Rottweiler to the vet. "My dog's cross-eyed: is there anything you can do for him?" "We'll see," says the vet. "Let's have a look at him." So he picks the dog up and has a good look at its eyes. "Hmm," says the vet, "I'm afraid I'm going to have to put him down." "Why? Because he's cross-eyed?"
"No, because he's extremely heavy..."

The newspaper seller was standing on the corner with a stack of papers, yelling, "Extra! Extra! Read all about it! Fifty people swindled! Fifty people swindled!" Curious, a man walked over, bought a paper, and checked the front page. Finding nothing, the man said, "There's nothing in here about 50 people being swindled!"
The newspaper seller just ignored him and went on, calling out, "Extra! Extra! Read all about it! Fifty-one people swindled!"

What happens to a hamburger that misses a lot of school?
He has to ketchup!

What's an indication of iron deficiency?
Wrinkly clothes!

The school head was very proud of his school's academic record. "It is very impressive," said one parent who was considering sending his son there. "How do you maintain such high standards?" "Simple," said the head. "The school motto says it all." "What's that?" asked the parent.
"If at first you don't succeed, you're expelled!"

A lady lost her handbag in the bustle of Christmas shopping.
It was found by an honest little boy and returned to her.
Looking in her purse, she commented, "That's funny. When I lost my bag there was a £20 note in it.
Now there are 20 pound coins!"
The boy replied, "That's right. The last time I found a lady's purse, she didn't have any change to give me a reward!"

Grandad: Look at my fantastic new hearing aid, Billy. It's made with the very latest technology developed from the US Space programme.
Billy: Wow! How does it work?
Grandad: Half past seven!

Piano Tuner: I've come to tune the piano.
Music Teacher: But we didn't send for you.
Piano Tuner: No, the people who live across the street did!

How did Bo Peep lose her sheep?
She had a crook with her!

What's Dracula's favourite Sc-Fi movie?
The Vampire Strikes Back!

A bloke was having some medical problems and his doctor told him that he had to drink warm water one hour before breakfast.
At the end of a week he returned and the doctor asked if he was feeling better. The man said that he actually felt worse.
"Did you drink warm water an hour before breakfast each day?"
"No," replied the man. "All I could manage was to drink for 20 minutes..."

Harry's very good for other people's health...
Whenever they see him coming, they go for a long walk!

What's grey and furry on the inside and white on the outside?
A mouse sandwich.

What happened to the man who brushed his teeth with gunpowder?
He kept shooting his mouth off!

Did you hear about the boy who was so ugly that his parents hired an actor
to play him in their home videos?

What is musical and handy in the supermarket?
A Chopin Liszt!

What do you call a girl lying on a tennis court?
Annette!

Why did the chewing gum cross the road?
It was stuck to the leg of a chicken!

What do you get if you cross an artist with a policeman?
A brush with the law!

Doctor, I've lost my memory.
When did this happen?
When did what happen?

What do you get if you cross a bear with a skunk?
Winnie-the-Pooh!

What do octopi play in their spare time?
Name that tuna!

What did the hedgehog say to the cactus?
"Is that you, Mum?"

Why did the tomato turn red?
It saw the salad dressing!

What did the grape do when it got stepped on?
It let out a little wine!

First cannibal: Come and have tea in our hut tonight.
Second cannibal: What are you having?
First cannibal: Hot buttered soldiers with hard-boiled legs!

How do you make a Kleenex dance?
Put a little boogey in it!

Where do bees go to the bathroom?
At the BP station!

My cat likes to sit down each evening and surf the internet.
Wow! what a smart animal!
Not really, it took the dog three weeks to teach him!

My uncle must be the meanest man in the world.
He found an old crutch in the street - then he broke his leg so he could use it!

What do snakes write on the bottom of their letters?
With love and hisses!

How does a mummy start a letter?
Tomb it may concern!

Last night I wrote myself a letter.
But I forgot to sign it and now I don't know who it's from!

Patient: Doctor, everyone thinks I'm a liar.
Doctor: Pull the other one!

What's the most important thing to remember in Chemistry?
Never lick the spoon!

A man went to the doctor to ask for help because he was feeling very tired and weak. The doctor prescribed some pills to make him feel better. A few days later the man went back to the surgery. "Are you feeling any stronger?" asked the doctor. "No," said the man,
"I can't get the lid off the bottle."

If King Kong went to Hong Kong to play ping pong and died, what would they put on his coffin?
A lid!

Did you hear about the ugly man who sent his picture to a lonely hearts club?
They sent it back saying they weren't that lonely!

A guy goes in to see a psychiatrist. He says,
"Doc, I can't seem to make any friends. Can you help me, you fat slob?"

What did the water say to the boat?
Nothing, it just waved!

Jim: What's white, steep, and has ears?
Tara: I don't know.
Jim: A snow-covered mountain!
Tara: What about the ears?
Jim: Haven't you ever heard of mountaineers?

A man is driving down a country road, when he spots a farmer standing in the middle of a huge field of grass. He pulls the car over to the side of the road and notices that the farmer is just standing there, doing nothing, looking at nothing. The man gets out of the car, walks all the way out to the farmer and asks him, "Er, excuse me mister, but what are you doing?" The farmer replies, "I'm trying to win a Nobel Prize."
"How?" asks the man, puzzled.
"Well, I heard they give the Nobel Prize to people who are out standing in their field."

Did you hear about the man who drank a bottle of lavatory cleaner?
He went clean round the bend!

A man comes into the rehearsal room of a big orchestra. He puts two large sacks on a table and says to the conductor, "Here you are, Sir. I managed to get some Nokias, a few Ericssons, some Motorolas..."
"You idiot," says the conductor,
"I told you to get two saxophones!"

A man in a restaurant is a little perturbed to see the waiter by his table scratching his bum. "Excuse me!" he said, "Have you got an itchy bottom?"
"No, Sir," said the waiter, "only what's on the menu."

Suffering from a bad case of the 'flu, a man phoned his doctor to get an appointment. The receptionist told him the earliest the doctor could see him was in three weeks' time. "Three weeks?" he shouted, "I could be dead by then!" The receptionist replied,
"In that case, could you get your wife to cancel the appointment?"

What's the difference between a fisherman and a schoolboy?
One baits hooks, the other hates books!

Farmer John: That pig is like one of the family.
Farmer Bob: Really? Which one?

What do you know when you see three elephants walking down the street wearing pink sweatshirts?
They're all on the same team!

What did one zombie say to another?
Get a life!

What is clown tea?
A brew ha-ha!

Who took ten thousand pigs up a hill?
The Grand Old Duke of Pork!

Did you hear about the man who picked his nose for 20 years?
His head caved in!

Two men were knocking in nails to the sides of a house and one of them kept throwing the nails over his shoulder. "Why do you keep throwing nails away?" said the other bloke. "Because they have the point at the wrong end," the first guy replied.
"You idiot!" said the first man, "We could use those on the other side of the house!"

What did the monster do to stop his son biting his nails?
He cut all his fingers off!

What did the fish say when he swam into the wall?
Dam!

Why don't skeletons fight?
They don't have the guts!

Which mythical creature makes the best footballer?
A centaur forward!

Quasimodo is sat in his study and once again is feeling depressed about how ugly he is. Looking for some reassurance, he goes in search of Esmerelda. When he finds her he asks her, once again, if he really is the ugliest man alive. Esmerelda sighs and says, "Look, why don't you go upstairs and ask the magic mirror who is the ugliest man alive? The mirror will answer your question once and for all." About five minutes later a very pleased looking Quasimodo bounced back down the stairs and gave Esmerelda a great big hug. "Well it worked," Quasmido beamed,
"but who is Chris Evans?"

Did you hear about the woman who was so keen on road safety that she always wore white at night?
She was run over by a snow plough.

What do you get if you cross a plumber with a field of cow pats?
The poohed piper!

What is a myth?
A female moth!

Did you hear about the mad scientist who put dynamite in his fridge?
He blew his cool!

What does one star say to another star when they meet?
Glad to meteor!

Have you heard about the Ellarwi, the lost tribe of Africa?
They run around shouting, "We're the Ellarwi?"

Why did the boy wear a belt on his teeth?
He couldn't find his braces!

How do you stop a snake from striking?
Pay it decent wages!

A man is feeling very ill, so he goes to see his doctor and is immediately rushed to hospital to undergo tests. The man wakes up after the tests in a private room at the hospital, and the phone by his bed rings. "This is your doctor. We've had the results back from your tests and we've found you have a really nasty disease, and it's very catching."
"Oh my God, doctor!
What are you going to do?"
"We're going to put you on a diet of pizzas, pancakes and pitta bread."
"Will that cure me?" said the man.
"Well no, but it's the only food we can get under the door!"

What do you give an elephant that's going to be sick?
Plenty of space!

What do you call a judge with no fingers?
Justice thumbs!

What's the best way to serve turkey?
Join the Turkish army!

What did the banana do when the monkey chased it?
The banana split!

What do you call a bad lion tamer?
Claude Bottom!

What's a haunted chicken?
A poultry-geist!

Uncle Charlie: You're very quiet, Fred.
Fred: Well, Mom gave me 10 cents not to say anything about your big hairy eyebrows!

The domestic science teacher was in a delicatessen buying nuts for the afternoon's cake baking.
"What kind of nuts would you like?" asked the salesgirl.
"Cashew," replied the teacher.
"Bless you," said the salesgirl. "What kind of nuts would you like?"

What do you get if you cross an octopus and a skunk?
An octopong!

What do you do with a blue whale?
Try to cheer him up!

Why do birds fly south for the winter?
Its quicker than walking!

A man is visiting a farm.The farmer takes him to a field. In the middle of the field is a six-legged chicken. "Good Lord!" says the man. "Where did you find that?" "We breed them that way specially," says the farmer. "You see, there are six of us in the family, and when we have a roast chicken, we all like a drumstick."
"That is extraordinary," says the man, "and what do they taste like?"
"I've no idea," says the farmer,
"we've never managed to catch one yet!"

Did you hear the joke about the roof?
Never mind, it's over your head!

What did the orange juice say to the water?
Diluted to meet you!

How did the midget get into the police force?
He lied about his height.

What did the ground say to the earthquake?
You crack me up!

What do you get when you cross a cow and a duck?
Cheese and quackers!

First vampire: Are you a light sleeper?
Second vampire: No, I sleep in the dark!

What happens if you eat yeast and shoe polish?
Every morning you'll rise and shine!

What do you call someone who is afraid of Santa?
Clausterphobic!

A new porter at a hotel in Paris was instructed by the manager that it was important to call the guests by their names, in order to make them feel welcome, and that the easiest way to find out their name was to look at their luggage.
Armed with this advice, the porter took two guests up to their rooms, put down their bags and said,
"I 'ope you 'ave a very 'appy stay 'ere in Paris, Mr and Mrs Real Leather."

Tiffany and Britney were talking in the corridor.
"That boy over there is getting on my nerves," said Tiffany.
"But he's not even looking at you," replied Britney.
"That's what's getting on my nerves," said Tiffany.

What starts with a P, ends with an E, and has a million letters in it?
Post Office!

Why did the boy sprinkle sugar on his pillow before he went to sleep?
So he could have sweet dreams!

What do you call cheese that is not yours?
Nacho Cheese!

The new office-boy came into his boss's office and nervously said,
"I think you're wanted on the phone, sir."
"What d'you mean, you think?" demanded the boss.
"Well, sir, the phone rang, I answered it and a voice said, 'Is that you, you smelly old fool?'"

Where is Dracula's American office?
The Vampire State Building.

What did the police officer say to his tummy?
You're under a vest!

What do you call a blond police officer?
A fair cop!

What's thick, black, floats on water and shouts "Dirty pants!"?
Crude oil!

Did you hear about the vampire who joined an orchestra?
He stood on the roof and conducted lightning!

What has one head, one foot and four legs?
A bed!

Why were the teacher's eyes crossed?
She couldn't control her pupils!

What did the judge say to the dentist?
I want you to pull the tooth, the whole tooth and nothing but the tooth!

A scientist cloned himself but the experiment created a twin who used terribly foul language.
As the clone cursed and swore, the scientist finally pushed it out of the window, and it fell to its death.
Later the scientist was arrested for making an obscene clone fall!

What sits in a tree and says "Hoots mon, hoots mon?"
A Scottish owl!

What does an educated owl say?
T'wit T'Whom!

Why did the owl 'owl?
Because the Woodpecker would peck 'er!

A man goes into a Post Office with some jelly stuck in one ear and some whipped cream stuck in the other.
The man behind the counter says. "Why have you got jelly in one ear and whipped cream in the other?"
The man says, "You'll have to speak up, I'm a trifle deaf!"

Joe comes home to his wife very upset. "The Doctor told me I've got to take these pills for the rest of my life," he tells her.
"That's not so bad," she says.
"It is. He only gave me six!"

Jack: Daddy, the vicar says we are here to help others...
Dad: That's absolutely right.
Jack: Then what are the others here for?

Sherlock Holmes and Dr Watson went on a camping trip. After a good meal cooked on the campfire, they lay down for the night and went to sleep. Some hours later, Holmes awoke and nudged his faithful friend. "Watson, look up at the sky and tell me what you see." Watson replied, "I see millions and millions of stars." "And what does that tell you?" enquired Holmes. Watson pondered for a minute. "Astronomically, it tells me that there are millions of galaxies and potentially billions of planets. Astrologically, I observe that Saturn is in Leo. I can also deduce from the position of the stars that the time is approximately a quarter past three. Meteorologically, I suspect that we will have a beautiful clear day tomorrow... What does it tell you, Holmes?" Holmes was silent for a minute, then spoke:
"Watson, you fool.
Someone has stolen our tent!"

Why couldn't the pirate play cards?
Because he was sitting on the deck!

A small boy was lost, so he went up to a policeman and said, "I've lost my Dad!" The policeman said, "What's he like?"
The little boy replied, "Beer and football!"

What do call a scary video about pasties?
A Cornish nasty!

What do you call crocodile photos?
Snapshots!

Two owls were playing pool. One said, "Two hits."
The other replied, "Two hits to who?"

A man walks into a bar with a newt on his shoulder. The barman looks at the creature and asks the man what he calls it. "Tiny," replies the man. "Why's that?" asks the barman.
"Because he's my newt!"

What's an Ig?
An Eskimo's house with no loo!

What do confused owls say?
Too-whit-to-why?

What's the difference between a vampire with toothache and a monsoon?
One roars with pain and the other pours with rain!

"I'd like a cheap parrot, please," an old lady said to a pet shop owner. "This one's cheap and it sings The Star-Spangled Banner."
"Never mind that," said the customer. "Is it tender?"

"How was your blind date?" a college student asked her roommate. "Terrible!" the roommate answered. "He turned up in his 1932 Rolls Royce." "Wow! That's a very expensive car. He sounds like a catch!"
"Not really, he was the original owner!"

Teacher: Stella, why do we put a hyphen in "bird-cage"?
Stella: For a parrot to perch on, miss.

The great Roman emperor Julius Caesar was watching Christians being thrown to the lions. "One good thing about this sport," he said to one of his generals,
"we never get pitch invasions."

What do you call a camel with three humps?
Humphrey!

"Sir!" said Alexander. "Empty Coke cans, hamburger cartons, plastic bags, used Kleenex, broken bottles, empty boxes..." "Do shut up, Alexander!" snapped the teacher.
"You're talking rubbish again!"

Two hunters, not the sharpest tools in the box, went duck hunting one morning with their dogs. After four hours with no success, Bobby says, "I know what we're doing wrong, Terry.
We're not throwing the dogs high enough."

Why did Tony go out with a prune?
Because he couldn't get a date!

What did Geronimo say when he jumped out of the airplane?
ME!!!

What training do you need to collect litter in the park?
None, you pick it up as you go along!

Two men were working on a construction site. When lunchtime came, one of them took out a box of sandwiches.
"Fish paste and tomato," he moaned, as he bit into the first.
"More fish paste and tomato," he muttered as he ate the second.
"Fish paste and tomato?" his friend asked as he picked up the third sandwich.
"Yes," sighed the man.
"I hate fish paste and tomato."
"Why don't you ask your wife to make you something different?"
The man looked at him strangely.
"I don't have a wife. I make them myself."

Two sheep meet on a country lane, the first one says, "Baa!"
The second one says, "Woof!"
"What are you up to? Sheep don't go 'Woof'," said the first sheep.
"I'm sorry," said the second,
"I'm new round here!"

Where does an Eskimo pig live?
In a Pigloo!

How do you make a sausage roll?
Give it a push!

Wife to Husband: I think Jordan may grow up to work for NASA.
I was talking to his teacher today and she said he was just taking up space!

Did you hear that Pinocchio got splinters in his fingers?
He'd been scratching his bum!

What happened to the entertainer who did a show for an audience of cannibals?
He went down really well!

What did the shy pebble say?
I wish I was a little boulder!

The transatlantic liner was experiencing particularly heavy weather, and Mrs Jones wasn't feeling well. "Would you care for some supper, ma'am?" asked the steward. "No, thanks," replied the wretched passenger,
"just throw it straight overboard and save me the trouble!"

What happens if you put a skeleton in a tumble drier?
He comes out bone dry!

My uncle has plastic teeth and a fibreglass leg.
That's nothing, my aunty's got a chest made of oak!

A snail starts a slow climb up the trunk of an apple tree. He is watched by a sparrow who can't help laughing and eventually says, "Don't you know there aren't any apples on the tree yet?" "Yes," said the snail,
"but there will be by the time I get up there!"

Patient: I've just been bitten by a snake on my arm!
Doctor: Which one?
Patient: I don't know, they all look the same to me!

Why did the elephant eat a sofa and two chairs?
He had a suite tooth!

It was a sweltering hot summer. The teacher came into the classroom wiping his brow and said, "Phew! Ninety-two today!"
"Happy birthday to you. Happy birthday to you . . ." sang the class.

Statistics say that one in three people is mentally ill.
So check your two best friends, and if they seem okay, it's you!

Patient: Doctor, I can't stand being three feet tall any longer.
Doctor: You'll just have to learn to be a little patient!

Henry is telling his friend about his holiday in Switzerland. "I bet the scenery was amazing," said his friend. "Not really," said Henry,
"I couldn't see a thing, there were all these mountains in the way!"

Are you superstitious?
No.
Good. Lend me £13!

Where would you weigh a pie?
Somewhere over the rainbow, weigh a pie! (way up high?)

What did the retired pirate say to his long-lost friend?
Long time no sea!

A man comes home from a night of drinking. As he falls through the doorway, his wife says, "What do you think you're doing, coming home half drunk?" The man replies,
"I'm sorry, love. I ran out of money!"

Did you hear about the sailor that was discharged from the submarine service?
He was caught sleeping with the windows open!

What do you do with a green monster?
Put it in the sun until it ripens!

Two television aerials got married....
The ceremony wasn't that great but the reception was amazing!

First Werewolf: Nerg.
Second Werewolf: Nerg, nerg, yug.
First Werewolf: Don't change the subject!

Patient: Doctor, I keep thinking I'm a moth.
Doctor: So why did you come to see me?
Patient: Well, I saw the light in the window...

What's worse than raining cats and dogs?
Hailing taxis!

A lady opens the door one day to a salesman with a suitcase full of stuff. "Good morning, Madam, can I interest you in some brushes?"
"No thank you," said the lady.
"Could you use some dusters, then?" he said. "No," said the lady.
"How about a mop and bucket, or any cleaning materials at all?" he said.
"No, I don't want any cleaning materials, I'm sorry."
"That's all right. The woman next door said you never used them."

Two men were remembering their wedding days. "It was dreadful," said Bert. "I got the most terrible fright."
"What happened?" asked Harry.
"I married her," replied Bert.

One night, Tim was walking home when, all of a sudden, a thief jumped on him. Tim and the thief began to wrestle. They rolled about on the ground and Tim put up a tremendous fight.
However, the thief managed to get the better of him and pinned him to the ground. The thief then went through Tim's pockets and searched him, but all the thief could find on Tim was 25 pence. The thief was so surprised at this that he asked Tim why he had bothered to fight so hard for 25p.
"Was that all you wanted?" Tim replied, "I thought you were after the 500 quid I've got in my shoe!"

A Frenchman walks into a bar with a colourful parrot on his shoulder. The bar-tender says, "Hey, that thing's great. Where'd you get him?" The parrot says,
"France. There's millions of them!"

A man is standing at a bus stop eating sausage and chips when a woman turns up with a dog. The dog is very excited at the smell of sausage and starts barking like crazy. "Shall I throw him a bit?" says the man.
"If you like," says the woman.
So he chucked the dog over a wall...

A mummy skunk has two children, whom she names "In" and "Out." One day, the child skunks go out to play in the forest as usual, but after a while, they become separated. Out comes back in and tells his mother that In has got himself lost. She takes him back outside and tells him to help her call for him.
They begin calling "In!" "In!"
Out ventures out of sight from his mother for a minute, then comes running back to her with In in tow. Mama skunk says, "Out! How did you find In?"
"Easy," Out says, "In stinked!"

What does an elf get in a cow field?
A pat on the head!

What's yellow and clicks?
A ballpoint banana!

Doctor, I think I'm going to die!
Nonsense, that's the last thing you'll do!

Teacher: Where was the Queen crowned?
Gary: On her head?

Why did Snoopy resign?
He didn't want to work for Peanuts any more!

This match won't light!
That's funny, it did this morning!

A young farmer, Barney, comes back from his first visit to the big city and presents his girlfriend with an enormous diamond ring. "Goodness, it's huge!" she grinned. "Is it real, Barney?"
"It had better be," said Barney, "otherwise I've been done out of two pounds!"

What do elves do after school?
Gnomework!

A man is in a hardware store where he spies a long metal cylindrical object. Not sure what it is, he asks an assistant who tells him that it is a thermos, and that it is used to keep hot things hot, and cold things cold.
The man is very excited about this and buys one. The next day at work, he pulls out his new thermos. One of his mates asks him what it is. He says, "It's a thermos. It keeps hot things hot and cold things cold."
The friend is very impressed and asks him what he has in his thermos. He replies,
"Spaghetti Bolognaise and Ice Cream."

What happens if you watch too many cartoons?
You get Disney spells!

What two days of the week start with the letter "T"?
Today and Tomorrow!

Where do bulls get their messages?
On a bull-etin board!

What kind of crackers do firemen like in their soup?
Firecrackers!

A car driving down a country road spluttered to a complete stop near a field filled with cows. The driver, getting out to see what was the matter, noticed a cow looking at him. "I believe it's your radiator," said the cow. The startled man ran to the nearest farmhouse and knocked on the door. "A cow just gave me advice about my car!" he shouted. "Did the cow have big black spots on it?" the farmer asked. "Yes it did," the man replied.
"Oh, that's Ethel," said the farmer. "Don't pay any attention to her. She doesn't know a thing about cars."

If you drop a yellow hat in the Red Sea, how does it come out?
Wet!

What do you get if you cross a pony and a detective?
Inspector Horse!

When do you stop at green and go at red?
When you're eating a watermelon!

What do you call artificial pasta?
Mockaroni!

Why did the cookie go to the hospital?
He felt crummy!

What do you call a parrot with boots on?
A walkie-talkie!

One day a postman on his rounds was greeted by a boy and a huge dog. The postman said to the boy, "Does your dog bite?" "No," replied the boy. Just then the huge dog bit the postman. The man yelled, "Hey! I thought you said your dog doesn't bite!" "He doesn't," replied the boy.
"That's not my dog!"

A man walks into a pub with a crocodile. "Do you serve Scottish people in here?" he asks the barman. "Of course, Sir," the barman replies.
"Good. A pint for me, then, please, and two Scottish people for the crocodile."

What's got eight legs and can fly long distances?
Four geese!

Dan: Please, Miss! How do you spell "ichael"?
Teacher: "Don't you mean "Michael"?
Dan: "No, I've written the "M" already!

Mum and Dad are in the iron and steel business. She does the ironing and he does the stealing!

Ronan Keating was bragging to his mates in a pub: "Last year I insured my voice with Lloyds of London for two million pounds."
An old man overheard and said, "What did you spend the money on?"

What do you get if you cross a mummy and a spaceship?
Tutankha-moon!

What do stupid kids do at Hallowe'en?
They carve a face on an apple and go bobbing for pumpkins!

A woman goes to the doctor with a twig growing out of her head. The doctor has a look at the growth. He's a bit puzzled, but he gives her some pills. Two weeks later she is back, and the twig has grown into a small branch with leaves on it. The doctor is still perplexed, but he gives her some different pills. A month later she's back again. Now the tree is fully grown, with blossoms and fruit, and round it is a grassy area with some rocks and a small waterfall.
"Aha!" says the doctor. "I know what it is. You've got a beauty spot!"

Little Sonia was shouting her prayers: "Please God, send me a new Barbie for my birthday!" Her mother, overhearing this, said, "Don't shout dear, God isn't deaf."
"No," said Sonia, "but Grandad is, and he's in the next room!"

What do you call a story about young horses?
A pony tail!

What do you call a ghost who haunts the town hall?
A night mayor!

A husband says to his wife "You always carry my photo in your handbag to the office. Why?" The wife says: "When there is a problem, no matter how impossible, I look at your picture and the problem doesn't seem so bad." The husband says, "You see, how great I am for you?!" And the wife replies,
"Yes, I see your picture and say to myself, 'What can possibly be worse than this?'"

Were you long in the hospital?
No, I was the same size that I am now!

What stories do big boats tell little boats?
Ferry tales!

What do you get if you cross a mountain and a baby?
A cry for Alp!

"I bought this piano two years ago and I still can't play it." "Your finding it difficult to learn, are you?"
"No, I can't get the lid open!"

Did you hear about the man who invented a gadget for seeing through walls?
He calls it a "window"!

A police officer stopped a hiker walking along the road carrying a sign which read "To Seattle." "What are you doing with that?" asked the police officer.
"I'm walking to Seattle," said the hiker, "and I don't want to get lost!"

On a shopping trip to the city a farmer bought a 24-piece jigsaw puzzle. He worked on it every night for two weeks. Finally, the puzzle was finished.
"Look what I've done, Bob,"
he said proudly to a visiting neighbour.
"That's a fine thing, Jethro.
How long did it take you?"
"Only two weeks," said Jethro.
"Never done a puzzle myself," Bob said.
"Is two weeks fast?"
"I'll say!" Jethro said,
"On the box it says
'From two to four years'."

Why was the broom late?
It over swept!

What wears glass slippers and weighs a ton?
Cinderelephant!

What do you call a mad baker?
A Doughnut!

Ding dong bell,
Pussy's down the well,
But we've put some disinfectant down
to cover up the smell!

A professor of astronomy was giving a lecture: "I predict the world will end in about thirty million years."
"What? How many?!!"
a man choked from the back of the room.
"Thirty million years," said the prof.
"Phew!" sighed the man in relief. "I thought you said thirTEEN million years."

John kept pestering his parents to buy a video recorder, but they said they couldn't afford one. One day John came home clutching a package containing a brand-new video recorder. "Wherever did you get the money to pay for that?" asked his father.
"It's all right, Dad," replied John,
"I swapped the TV for it!"

This bloke bursts into the house and yells, "Pack your bags, Love, I've just won the lottery: ten million pounds!"
His wife says, "Wonderful! Should I pack for the beach or the mountains?"
He responds, "I don't care where you go, just get the heck out!"

Billy asked the bus driver how much it would cost to travel into town. "80 pence," said the driver. Billy didn't have enough, so he decided to run after the bus for a few stops. "How much is it now?" he asked, two stops later. "Still 80 pence," said the driver. Billy ran after the bus for another three stops and, panting, he asked "How much now?"
The driver replied, "90 pence.
You're going the wrong way!"

What does a witch get if she's a poor traveller?
Broom sick!

Who's the unluckiest man in the world?
The deep sea diver coming up who met his ship going down!

Tom: How awful that your Aunt drowned in a tub of varnish!
Harry: Yes, but what a finish!

Why did the cannibal go on a vegetarian diet?
He went off people!

What eats its victims two by two?
Noah's Shark!

How do monsters count to a thousand?
On their warts!

What happened at the cannibal's wedding party?
They toasted the bride and groom!

What do you get if you cross a werewolf with a hyena?
I don't know, but if it laughs I'll join in!

First zombie: Do you still hold your girlfriend's hand?
Second zombie: Yes, but I wish the rest of her would visit more often.

What did the zombie's friend say when he introduced him to his girlfriend?
Good grief! Where did you dig her up from?

Why did Tommy throw the clock out of the window?
Because he wanted to see time fly!

Have you ever seen a duchess?
Yes, it's the same as an English "S"!

What did the mother elf tell the baby elf when he ate too fast?
Stop goblin your food!

What do Dutch pet shop owners have on toast?
Hamster jam!

Tim: Did you hear about the idiot who keeps going around saying "No"?
Barney: No.
Tim: Oh, so it's you!

"There's trouble with the car," said the wife. "It has water in the carburettor."
"Water in the carburettor?" replied the husband. "That's ridiculous."
"I tell you, the car has water in the carburettor."
"You don't even know what a carburettor is!" said the husband. "I'll check it out. Where's the car?"
"It's in the canal."

Have you ever seen a Man-eating Tiger?
No, but in the café next door I once saw a man eating chicken!

An American tourist was visiting a quaint country village, and got talking to an old man in the local pub. "And have you lived here all your life, Sir?" asked the American.
"Not yet," said the villager.

Tom: They're not going to grow bananas any longer.
Tim: Really? Why not?
Tom: Because they're long enough already!

Mum: Why do you eat so fast?
Kid: I want to eat as much as possible before losing my appetite!

Jack: Would you like some Egyptian Pie?
Jill: What's Egyptian pie?
Jack: You know, the kind mummy used to make!

What did the tie say to the hat?
You go on ahead and I'll hang around here!

Waiter, this soup tastes funny.
Then why aren't you laughing?

Why did the belt go to jail?
Because it held up a pair of trousers!

What do you call an American drawing?
A Yankee Doodle!

What happened when two American stoats got married?
They became the United Stoats of America!

Why can't your nose be twelve inches long?
Because then it would be a foot!

Patient: Doctor, I've just swallowed the film from my camera!
Doctor: Well, let's hope nothing develops!

What is large, yellow, lives in Scotland and has never been seen?
The Loch Ness Canary!

A bloke goes to the barber and asks for a haircut like Ricky Martin. Ten minutes later, his hair is a disaster area, shaved bald down the middle with tufts on either side. The bloke gasps as he sees himself in the mirror. "Ricky Martin doesn't have his hair cut like this!" he protested.
"He would if he came in here," said the barber.

What's Irish and sits in the sun?
Paddy O'Furniture!

How do you tickle a rich girl?
Say "Gucci Gucci Gucci!"

What do you call a boomerang that doesn't work?
A stick!

Why are there so many Smiths in the phone book?
They all have phones!

A policeman sees a small boy in a pub drinking a pint of beer and smoking. "Hey! Why aren't you at school?" he says.
"I don't have to go to school," says the kid. "I'm only four."

Dad: How would you like a new bike for Christmas, son?
Son: I don't need one, Dad. I found one behind the wardrobe this morning!

Tony left Athens and moved to New York. He got a job through relatives who taught him to say "Apple pie and coffee" in English so he could order in a restaurant. The next day Tony walked into a diner. "What'll you have?" asked the waitress. "Apple pie anna coffee," said Tony. Since that was all he could say, he was forced to eat apple pie and coffee every day for a month. When he complained to his relatives, they taught him to say "Ham sandwich." Armed with his new vocabulary, Tony told the waitress, "Ham sandwich!" "White bread or brown?" she asked.
"Apple pie anna coffee?" replied Tony.

How do you cut through a fossil?
With a dinosaw!

How does a bird with a broken wing manage to land safely?
With a sparrowchute!

What do you call a space magician?
A flying sorcerer!

An Englishman, an Irishman and a Scotsman were in a pub, talking about their sons. "My son was born on St George's Day," commented the Englishman, "so we obviously decided to call him George." "That's a real coincidence," remarked the Scot. "My son was born on St Andrew's Day, so obviously we decided to call him Andrew." "That's incredible, what a coincidence," said the Irishman.
"Exactly the same thing happened with my son, Pancake."

Snow White received a camera for Christmas. She happily took pictures of the Dwarves and their little house. When she had finished she took the film to the shop to be developed. After a week or so she went to get the finished pictures. The shop assistant said the photos were not back from the processor. Snow White was disappointed and started to cry. The assistant, trying to console her, said,
"Don't worry. Some day your prints will come."

Mrs Johnson asked the class to write a composition about what they would do if they had a million dollars. Everyone except Fannie began to write. Fannie twiddled her thumbs and looked out of the window. When Mrs Johnson collected the papers, Fannie's sheet was blank. "Fannie," said Mrs. Johnson, "everyone has written two pages or more, but you've done nothing. Why is that?"
"Nothing is what I'd do," replied Fannie, "if I had a million dollars."

Young Bobby was being fitted for glasses, and his father, standing beside him, said,
"Now, remember, son. Don't wear them when you're not looking at anything!"

What's a cold, evil candle called?
The wicked wick of the north!

Two drunks are walking home and one says, "What a beautiful moon!" The other replies, "That's not the Moon, that's the Sun." They argue until they pass another drunk. "Hey! Can you tell us what's up in the sky? Is it the Moon or the Sun?" The third drunk looks at the sky and says,
"Sorry, I don't live around here!"

What do you get hanging from apple trees?
Sore arms!

What goes up when the rain comes down?
An umbrella!

What did the big firecracker say to the little firecracker?
My pop is bigger than yours!

Mother: Keep that dog out of the house, it's full of fleas.
Son: Keep out of the house, Fido, it's full of fleas!

A man walks into a doctor's office. He has a cucumber up his nose, a carrot in his right ear and a banana in his left ear. "What's the matter with me?" he asks the doctor. The doctor replies,
"You're not eating properly."

Dentist: Try to relax. I'll pull that aching tooth out in five minutes.
Patient: How much will this cost?
Dentist: It'll be £100.
Patient: That much for just five minutes' work?
Dentist: Well if you prefer, I can pull it out very slowly...

An insurance salesman was teaching his wife to drive when the brakes suddenly failed on a steep hill. "I can't stop!" she screamed. "What shall I do?"
"Brace yourself," advised her husband, "and try to hit something cheap!"

What do horses play when they're bored?
Stable tennis!

Doctor, I can't pronounce the letters "f" and "t"!
Well, you can't say fairer than that!

What do snakes do after they fight?
They hiss and make up!

A man whose son had just passed his driving test went home one evening and found that the boy had driven slap into the living room. "How did you manage to do that?" he fumed.
"Quite simple, Dad. I came in through the kitchen and turned left!"

What do you get if you cross a biscuit with an elephant?
Crumbs!

A woman walked into the bank to repay a loan. She had a £5 note stuck in one ear and a £10 note in the other.
That's right, she was £15 in arrears!

Mr and Mrs Smith were always fighting. Then one morning as Mrs Snith was going to the bank she was knocked down by a hit and run driver. A police officer rushed up and asked her if she'd taken the car's number. "I didn't need to," replied Mrs Smith. "It was my husband in that car." "Did you see him?" asked the officer.
"No," said Mrs Smith, "but I'd know that laugh anywhere!"

Did you hear about the Irish schoolboy who was studying Greek Mythology? When the teacher asked him to name something that was half-man and half-beast he replied,
"Buffalo Bill."

What do you call a group of chess fanatics bragging about their games in a hotel reception area?
Chess nuts boasting in an open foyer!

What kind of flower do you have between your nose and your chin?
Tulips!

A man went into a post office to see if there were any letters for him. "I'll see, sir," said the clerk. "What is your name?"
"Don't be silly," said the man. "My name will be on the envelope!"

Doctor: Now, tell me how you happened to burn both your ears.
Patient: I was doing the ironing when the telephone rang, and I picked up the iron and put that to my ear by mistake.
Doctor: But you've burnt both your ears!
Patient: That's right, I burned the other one ringing for the ambulance!

Why do surgeons wear masks?
If somebody makes a mistake, nobody will know who did it!

"You never get anything right!" complained the teacher. "What kind of job do you think you'll get when you leave school?"
"Well," said Tony, "I want to be the weatherman on TV."

A young chap rings on Mr Brown's door. "Good morning, sir. I'm applying for the job as handyman." "I see," said Mr Brown. "Well, are you handy?
"Couldn't be more so. I only live next door."

Customer: Hi. I'm looking for a good buy...
Salesman: Oh. OK. Goodbye!

Three weeks after her wedding day, Joanna called her mother on the phone. "Mum!" she wailed, "John and I had a REALLY bad fight!" "Calm down, love," said her mum, "it's not half as bad as you think. Every couple has a first fight." "I know, I know," said Joanna,
"but what am I going to do with the BODY?"

Emma said to Aunty Edna, "Blimey, you're ugly, aren't you?" Her mum overheard this and pulled Emma into the kitchen. "You naughty girl!" she screamed. "How can you say to your aunty that she's ugly? You go in and tell her you're sorry!" Emma went back to the living room, and said to her aunt,
"Aunt Edna, I'm sorry you're so ugly."

What's orange and flies?
Supercarrot!

A blind man was waiting to cross the road when a dog stopped and cocked its leg against him. The blind man felt in his pocket for a sweet, bent down, and offered it to the dog. A passer-by remarked what a very kind act that was considering what the dog had done.
"Not really," said the blind man, "I only wanted to find out which end to kick!"

Patient: Doctor, I keep thinking I'm my own cat.
Doctor: How long have you thought this?
Patient: Oo, ages. Since I was a kitten.

"Is ink very expensive, Dad?"
"No, son, what makes you ask that?"
"Well, I spilt some on the lounge carpet, and Mum went bananas!"

Postman 1: A dog bit me on the leg this morning.
Postman 2: Did you put anything on it?
Postman 1: No, he seemed to like it plain!

Why did the man with one hand cross the road?
To get to the second hand shop!

Why is Britain so wet?
Because the Queen has reigned there for 50 years!

Why do fish live in salt water?
Because pepper makes them sneeze!

What do you get when you cross a moose and a ghost?
A Cari-boo!

Wife: Shall I put the kettle on?
Husband: No, I think you look fine in the dress you're wearing!

What did Cinderella Seal wear to the ball?
Glass flippers!

What do you get if you cross a compass and a shellfish?
A guided mussel!

How does a flea get from place to place?
By itch-hiking!

How do you stop an elephant from going through the eye of a needle?
Tie a knot in its tail!

Two idiots go fishing. They catch a lot of fish and return to the shore.
1st idiot: I hope you remember the spot where we caught all those fish.
2nd idiot: Yes, I made an 'X' on the side of the boat to mark the spot.
1st idiot: You idiot! How do you know we'll get the same boat?

First cannibal: I don't know what to make of my husband these days.
Second cannibal: How about a curry?

A man and his rhinoceros were driving down the road when a police car pulled him over.
The policeman asked the man, "Didn't you know it is against the law to drive with a rhinoceros in the front seat of your car?"
The man replied, "No, I didn't know that." The policeman asked the man where he was going and he said, "To London." The policeman said, "I will let you off this one time if you promise to take this rhinoceros straight to the zoo when you get there."
So the man promised he would. Several days later the policeman spotted the man with the rhinoceros driving down the road and he pulled him over again. The policeman said, "I thought I told you to take this rhinoceros straight to the zoo?" And the man said,
"I did! He loved it!
We're going to the cinema now."

Waiter, waiter! There's a dead fly in my soup.
Yes sir, it's the heat that kills them.

What do you call a short vampire?
A pain in the knee!

What do you get if you cross a labrador and a tortoise?
A dog that will run to the shop and bring back last week's paper!

Two men were painting a house.
Pat: Have you got a good hold on that paint brush, Mick?
Mick: Yes, I have, Pat.
Pat: Good, because I'm taking this ladder away.

One day, a hungry and sad-looking man walked into a restaurant, and said to the waitress who came up to take his order, "I would like some stew please, and a few kind words." The waitress went away for a few minutes and then returned with a plate of stew which she placed before the customer. "That's my order all right," said the man, smiling.
"Now, do you have a few kind words?"
"Yes." whispered the waitress.
"Don't eat the stew!"

Why did the lion feel sick after he'd eaten the nicest man in the village?
Because it's hard to keep a good man down!

How do you make a skeleton laugh?
Tickle his funny bone!

What has four eyes but can't see?
Mississippi!

What did the gardener say when he saw his idiot assistant laying the lawn at a new house?
Green side up, Billy!

What gives us milk and only has one horn?
A milk lorry!

What kind of a car does an egg drive?
A Yolkswagon!

Why did the toilet paper roll down the hill?
To get to the bottom!

Which is the most dangerous animal in Tibet?
Yak the Ripper!

If athletes get athlete's foot, what do astronauts get?
Missiletoe!

Why did the Mexican throw his wife out the window?
He wanted tequila!

Mother: Did you get a good place in the geography test?
Fred: Yes, Mum, I sat next to the cleverest kid in the class!

Little Johnny and his mother were on a train. Johnny leant over and started to whisper in his mother's ear.
"Johnny, how many times have I told you?" said his mother. "It's rude to whisper. If you have something to say, say it out loud."
"All right," said Johnny.
"Why is that lady opposite so fat?"

Cross Purposes

What do you get if you cross a shark with a parrot?

An animal that talks your head off!

See if you can complete your own Cross Gags by picking an item from Box 1 and crossing it with something from Box 2. You should be able to make up all the weird stuff in Box 3 with your crosses!

A

A box of matches
A road
A sheep
A pig
A fat golfer
A cow
An artist

B

Tight trousers
A policeman
A grass cutter
A naked person
A giant
A safari park
A space ship

Polly wants a very
big cracker

The big match!
Double yellow lions!
Apollo neck jumper!
Streaky bacon!
A lawn mooer!
A brush with the law!
A hole in one!

Just before the Ark set sail, Noah saw his two sons fishing over the side. "Go easy on the bait, lads," he said.
"Remember I've only got two worms."

What is green and slimy and is found at the North Pole?
A lost frog.

What sings, dances, and lights up at night?
Jennifer Glowpez!

Two cows are standing in a field. One says, "Moo," and the other one says,
"I was about to say that!"

What do you call a line of rabbits walking backwards?
A receding Hare line!

What do you get if you cross a donkey and Christmas?
Muletide greetings!

Fred: Did you go to Betty's party?
Harry: No, the invitation said "from five to nine," and I'm ten!

A woman walked into a pet shop and said, "I'd like a frog for my son."
"Sorry, madam," said the manager, "we don't do part exchange."

Jacko: I was the teacher's pet last year.
Jono: Why was that?
Jacko: She couldn't afford a dog.

What did Adam say on the day before Christmas?
It's Christmas, Eve!

Why do babies walk softly?
Because they can't walk hardly!

What's the biggest thing ever made from fruit?
The grape wall of China!

Adam to Eve before the guests arrive:
"Darling, did you put my pants in the salad again?"

Bill and Doug went into a restaurant that looked a bit grubby. The waitress came over and asked if they wanted some menus.
"Er, no thanks," said Doug, "I'll just have a cup of black coffee."
"I'll have black coffee too," Bill said. "And please make sure the cup is clean."
The waitress turned and marched off into the kitchen. Two minutes later, she was back.
"Two cups of black coffee," she announced.
"Which one of you wanted the clean cup?"

In what month do dogs bark least?
In February, it's the shortest month!

What's small and cuddly and bright purple?
A koala holding his breath!

A policeman visits his mother; he knocks on the door and his Mum shouts: "Who is it?" and the policeman says,
"It's Me Ma, Me Ma, Me Ma!"

What do you call a young turkey?
A goblet!

Girl: Did you like that cake, Mrs Jones?
Mrs Jones: Yes, very much.
Girl: That's funny. My Mum said you didn't have any taste!

What did the kids say when they saw Dr. Jekyll coming?
Hyde! It's Dr. Jekyll!

What does a spy do when it rains?
He goes undercover!

How do you change tyres on a duck?
With a quackerjack!

A huge American car screeched to a halt in a sleepy English village, and the driver called out to a local chap, "Say, am I on the right road for William Shakespeare's house?"
"Ay, straight on, sir," said the man, "but no need to hurry. He's dead."

Do you know a bloke with one leg called Ben Smith?
No. What's his other leg called?

What do you call two Quidditch players on one broom?
Broommates!

What do you call a writer who plays snooker with two pints on her head?
Beatrix Potter!

A rather stern aunt had been staying with Angela's parents, and one day she said to the little girl, "Well, Angela, I'm going tomorrow. Are you sorry?"
"Oh yes, Auntie," replied Angela, "I thought you were going today."

Tim once took his little sister with him while he went fishing. When he returned, he was looking very fed up. "I'll never do that again," he complained to his Dad. "Did she frighten off the fish?" enquired Dad. "No," replied Tim.
"She ate all my maggots."

Retired colonel: Ever hunted bear, son?
Grandson: No, but I've been fishing in my shorts!

What did the stamp say to the envelope?
Stick with me and we'll go places!

What do you get if you cross a tortoise and a storm?
A not in a hurry cane!

Jack: Did you hear about the giant that threw up?
Jill: No, how'd you know?
Jack: It's all over town!

A police officer saw a man dressed as a cowboy in the street, complete with huge stetson hat, spurs, and six shooters.
"Excuse me, sir," said the police officer, "who are you?"
"The name's Tex, officer," said the cowboy.
"Ah, You're from Texas?" said the police officer,
"Nope, Louisiana."
"Louisiana? So why are you called Tex?"
"Well, I don't want to be called Louise."

First cannibal: My dad's so tough he can kill a man by blinking his eyes.
Second cannibal: My dad's so tough it took Mum six hours to cook him in the microwave!

Doctor, I think my eyesight is getting worse!
I think it is. This is a Post Office!

Why should you take a pencil to bed?
In case you want to draw the curtains!

Why should you listen to a qualified American coinsmith?
He makes perfect cents!

What part of a fish weighs the most?
The scales!

Doctor: It's bad news, I'm afraid. You've only got four minutes to live.
Patient: But doctor, isn't there anything you can do for me?
Doctor: Well, I could boil you an egg!

See my cat? He's just drunk 83 saucers of milk.
That must be a lap record!

A wild west gunman is being lead away by the county sheriff. "Say, do I really have to die swinging from a tree?" "Course not," replied the Sheriff. "We just put the rope round your neck and kick the horse away. After that it's up to you!"

What sort of star is dangerous?
A shooting star!

Which month do soldiers hate most?
The month of March!

What did the painter say to the wall?
One more crack like that and I'll plaster you!

What is white and goes up?
Stupid snow!

A salesman dropped in to see a business customer. No one was in the office except a big dog emptying wastebaskets. The salesman stared at the animal, wondering if his imagination could be playing tricks on him. The dog looked up and said, "Don't be surprised. This is just part of my job." "Incredible!" exclaimed the man. "I can't believe it! Does your boss know what a prize he has in you, an animal that can talk?" "Don't tell him that!" said the dog. "If he finds out I can talk, he'll make me answer the phone as well!"

What are two things you cannot have for breakfast?
Lunch and dinner!

What do you call a crate of ducks?
A box of quackers!

Two country boys were in London. Ben turns to Jethro and says: "Ben, look at that shop over there, I thought London was supposed to be expensive but that shop is as cheap as chips!"
Ben says: "You're right! Suits £10.00, Shirts £4.00, Trousers £5.00, I think that we should buy a load and take them back to the country. We would make a tidy profit selling those alright!"
Jethro says, "Wait though, the shopkeeper will never let us have them if he thinks that we're going export them to the country and make our fortune..."
Ben thinks and says: "I've got idea! You can do the best Cockney accent. You go in there and do the talking and I'll just stand behind you and say nothing. He'll never guess we're country boys!"
The boys go into the shop, where Jethro does his best London accent:
"Awwight Guvnor, I'll 'ave 20 of yer 'Whistle 'un Flutes', 20 'Dickie Dirts' and 20 pairs of 'Strides'. And if yer don't mind I'll be paying with the 380 'Pictures of the Queen' in my 'Sky Rocket'."
The owner smiles and asks,
"You're country boys aren't you?"
Quite bemused, Jethro replies,
"How did you work that one out?"
The Owner replies,
"This is a Dry Cleaners, mate."

What do you get if you cross a computer with a potato?
Micro chips!

"Your students must miss you a lot," said the woman in the next bed to the teacher in hospital.
"Not at all. Their aim's usually good. That's why I'm here!"

What do you get if you cross a jogger with an apple pie?
Puff pastry!

One day, a little girl was sitting and watching her mother do the dishes at the kitchen sink. She suddenly noticed that her mother had several strands of white hair sticking out among her brown locks. The little girl looked at her mother and inquisitively asked, "Why are some of your hairs white, Mum?"
Her mother replied, "Well, every time you do something wrong and make me cry or unhappy, one of my hairs turns white."
The little girl thought about this for a while and then said,
"Wow, you must have been awful to Granny!"

What do you get if you cross an Italian landmark and a ghost?
The screaming tower of Pisa!

A stupid man was struggling out of his house with a big table. His neighbour said to him, "Hello, Harry. Where are you going with that then?" And Harry replied,
"I'm taking it to the shop to have it measured for a new tablecloth."

What do you call it when a frog takes a shower?
Spring cleaning!

Tourist: How do I get to the London Palladium?
Musician: Practise.

What is the best material for kites?
Fly paper!

What did Dick Turpin say after riding from London to York?
"Whoa!"

What is an asset?
A small donkey!

What's big and green and sits in a corner?
The Incredible Sulk!

What's curly and yellow and hangs about?
A drip dry banana!

Ah, Doctor Watson. You're wearing your winter underwear!
Good Lord, Holmes! How on Earth did you deduce that?
You've forgotten to put your trousers on again!

Who is always let down by his mates?
A deep sea diver!

Fred: Is that a new perfume I smell?
Betty: Yes it is, and yes, you do!

What do you call a wizard that doesn't want to be late?
Hurry Potter!

A man walks into a club and asks for a drink. The barman refuses because the man has already had one too many. So the man says "OK then, can I play darts instead?" The barman says, "No way! You could have someone's eye out in your condition!" The man replied, "Just give me one chance. If I miss, I'll leave." The barman agrees, just to get rid of him. The man throws the dart and hits the bull's-eye. The barman says "Congratulations! You have won first prize!" So the man says, "What's my prize?" The bartender had bought a pet turtle for his son, so he gave that to the man. The man goes home and comes back the next day. There is a different barman there that night, and the man is as drunk as he'd been the night before, so when he asks if he can play darts, the barman refuses. The man says, "But I won first prize yesterday!" The barman asks "What was your prize?" The man replies, "A hamburger!"

How do you know when an elephant has been in your fridge?
Enormous footprints in the butter!

A man died and his wife phoned the newspaper to place an obituary. She called the obituary department and said, "This is what I want to print: 'Bernie is dead'." The man at the newspaper said, "But for £10 you're allowed to print seven words." The woman answered:
"OK. Then print: 'Bernie is dead. Ford Escort for sale'."

A salesman goes up to a house and rings the doorbell. A very small boy answers the door with a big fat cigar in one hand and a large glass of whisky in the other. "Is your Mum or Dad in?" says the salesman.
"Does it look like it?" says the boy.

What do you get if you cross a motorcycle and a funny story?
A Yamahahaha!

What did the fireman's wife get for Christmas?
A ladder in her stocking!

How did the farmer mend his pants?
With cabbage patches!

How do you repair a broken tomato?
With Tomato Paste!

Why did the baby strawberry cry?
Because his parents were in a jam!

Why didn't the chicken cross the road?
He was chicken!

One day Will's girlfriend wrote to him to say their relationship was off and could she have her photograph back? Will sent her a pile of pictures of different girls with the message:
I can't remember what you look like. Could you please take out your photo and return the rest?

Patient: Doctor, you have to help me stop talking to myself!
Doctor: Why is that?
Patient: I'm a salesman, I keep selling myself things I don't want!

Psychiatrist: Well, what's your problem?
Patient: I prefer brown shoes to black shoes.
Psychiatrist: There's nothing wrong with that. Lots of people prefer brown shoes to black shoes. I do myself.
Patient: Really? How do your like yours - fried or boiled?

What do you call a TV programme about a load of sheep?
A flockumentary!

Three grannies were walking down the road. They were all a bit deaf.
"It's windy," said the first.
"No, it's Thursday," said the second.
The third one said, "I'm thirsty too. Let's have a cup of tea!"

What kind of key opens the door at Christmas?
A turkey!

What do you get if you cross two bees and a coach?

A double decker buzz!

At our local restaurant you can eat dirt cheap.

But who wants to eat dirt?

Once upon a time there was a Prince who was cast under a spell by an evil witch. The curse was that the Prince could speak only one word each year. However, he could save up the words so that if he did not speak for a whole year, the following year he was allowed to speak two words. One day he met a beautiful princess and fell madly in love. With the greatest difficulty he decided not to speak for two years so that he could look at her and say "My darling." But at the end of the two years he decided he wanted to say "I love you" as well, so he waited another three years. But at the end of these three years he realised that he had to ask her to marry him too. So he waited another four years without speaking. Finally, after nine years, the day arrived. Leading the lovely princess to the most secluded and romantic place in that beautiful royal garden, the prince heaped 100 red roses on her lap, knelt before her, and taking her hand in his, said, "My darling, I love you! Will you marry me?" The princess tucked a strand of golden hair behind a dainty ear, opened her sapphire eyes in wonder, and, parting her ruby lips, said:

"Pardon?"

What do you call a cow with no sense of direction?

Udderly lost!

Why is a self-employed person not like Robinson Crusoe?
Because Robinson Crusoe got all his work done by Friday!

**One day a very old lady said to her very old husband, "Norman, will you please go to the kitchen and get me a bowl of ice cream? And why don't you write that down so you won't forget?"
"Don't be daft, woman," said the husband, "I can remember a bowl of ice cream!"
"Well," said the wife, "I'd also like some strawberries on it. You'd better write that down, because you know you'll forget."
"Don't be silly," replied the husband, "a bowl of ice cream and some strawberries. I can remember that!"
"OK, dear, but I'd like you to put some whipped cream on top. Now you'd really better write it down now. You'll forget," said the wife.
"Come now, my memory's not that bad!" said the husband. "No problem, a dish of ice cream with strawberries and whipped cream." He came back from the kitchen about 15 minutes later with a plate of bacon and eggs. The wife took one look at the plate, glanced up at her husband and said,**
"What happened to the toast?"

What happened at the badly organised cow-milking contest?
It was udder chaos...

Doctor, my son has swallowed my pen. What should I do?
Use a pencil till I get there!

What is a calf after it is one year old?
Two years old!

"Can you read the top line of letters on the chart?" said the optician.
"No," said the man.
"How about the second line, can you read that?" said the optician.
"No," said the man.
"Can you read the bottom line, then?" said the optician.
"No, I can't read at all."

A man goes into a clothes shop. "Can I try on that suit in the window?" he said. The assistant replies,
"No, use the changing room like everyone else!"

A drunk man staggered up to the hotel reception and demanded that he be changed to a different room.
"But sir," said the receptionist, "you already have the best room in the hotel."
"I inshisht on another room!" slurred the man.
"Very well, sir. I'll change you from 502 to 555. But would you mind telling me exactly what's wrong with room 502?" asked the clerk.
"Well, for one thing," said the man, "it'sh on fire."

Did you hear about the man who believed in reincarnation?
In his will he left his money to himself.

What does a newt cover his shower with?
Rep-tiles!

What's the difference between Harry Potter going on holiday and a fat duck coming in to land?
One packs the wand and the other whacks the pond!

Why did the birdie go to the hospital?
To get tweetment!

Glen: My Gran knitted me three socks for my birthday...
Sally: Why three socks?
Glen: Because I wrote and told her that I'd grown another foot!

A vicar is walking down the street one day when he notices a boy trying to press a doorbell on a house across the street. However, the boy is very small, and the doorbell is too high for him to reach. After watching the boy's efforts for some time, the vicar decides to help. He crosses the street, walks up behind the little fellow and, placing his hand kindly on the child's shoulder, leans over and gives the doorbell a solid ring. The child looks over his shoulder and grins.
"Nice one Vicar," he says.
"Now run for it!"

Teacher: What did Julius Caesar say to Brutus when Brutus stabbed him?
Emma: Ow!

Did you hear about the scientist who invented an acid that could burn through anything?
He can't find anything to keep it in!

Mum, Can I have a dog for Christmas?
No, you can have turkey like everyone else!

A mountaineer fell down a very deep crevasse, breaking both his arms. Another member of the party managed to lower a rope until it was just within reach of the man's head. "Quick!" he shouted. "Get hold of the rope with your teeth and I'll pull you up." Inch by painful inch, the mountaineer was dragged back up the crevasse. When he had only two feet to go, his rescuer called out, "Are you all right?"
"Yes-aaaaaaaaargh!!" came the reply.

Did you hear about the girl who met the boy in a revolving door?
They've been going round together ever since!

Two fleas were sitting on Robinson Crusoe's back as he lay on the beach in the sun.
"Well, I'm off," said one to the other, "I'll see you on Friday!"

Mummy, what's a vampire?
Be quiet, dear, and drink your soup before it clots!

A film producer tells an actor "Great news! I'm giving you the star part in my next movie. It's Treasure Island, and you're Long John Silver. You're on £20,000 a week and you start next Tuesday!"
"Fantastic!" said the actor, "For 20 grand a week, why can't I start on Monday?"
"No can do," the producer says, "Monday we're cutting your leg off."

Doctor: Please breathe out three times.
Patient: Are you checking my lungs?
Doctor: No. I want to clean my glasses!

What do you call a spaceship in a chip pan?
An Unidentified Frying Object!

Patient: Doctor, I've broken my arm in two places.
Doctor: Well don't go back to those places again!

How do you poison a woman with a pair of scissors?
Give her arsenic!

Danny: What did you get for Christmas?
Donny: A trumpet. It's the best present I ever got!
Danny: Why?
Donny: My Mum pays me a fortune not to play it!

What's the difference between a sprinter and a duck?
One goes quick on its legs, the other goes quack on its legs!

What language do they speak in Cuba?
Cubic!

A termite walks into a bar and asks,
"Is the bar-tender here?"

A skeleton walks into this bar.
He orders a beer and a mop!

A man goes to the doctor with a strawberry growing out of his head.
The Doctor says, "I'll give you some cream to put on that."

What did Delaware when Mississippi lent Missouri her New Jersey?
I don't know, Alaska!

In what school do you learn how to greet people?
Hi school!

Why did the cannibal live on his own?
He was fed up with other people!

Doctor, I can't get to sleep...
Sit on the edge of the bed, you'll soon drop off!

Why did the man take off his door bell?
He wanted to win the No Bell prize!

Victoria: Did you know they're not making pencils any longer?
David: Wow! Why not?
Victoria: They're already long enough!

There were two mosquitoes watching donors giving their blood.
"Isn't that typical?" said one to the other.
"They're quite happy to lie there and let someone suck a whole pint of blood out of them, but if you nip in for a tiny sip they try to kill you!"

This fellow is looking to buy a saw to cut down some trees in his garden. He goes to a chainsaw shop and asks about various chainsaws. The dealer tells him, "This chainsaw here is fantastic, it will cut down 100 trees in one day." So, the man takes the chainsaw home and begins working on the trees. After cutting for several hours he's still cut down only two trees. He gives up. The next day he gets up at dawn and cuts all day, but he still only manages three trees. He is really fed up. The next day the man takes the saw back to the dealer and explains the problem. The dealer, baffled by the man's claim, removes the chainsaw from the case. The dealer says, "Hmm, it looks fine." Then the dealer starts the chainsaw's engine up, and the man says,
"What's that noise?"

What do you get if you cross a carrier pigeon with a woodpecker?
A bird that knocks before delivering the post!

A Canadian logging company advertises for a lumberjack. A skinny little chap shows up at the camp the next day carrying an axe. The head lumberjack takes one look at the puny little fellow and tells him to get lost.
"Give me a chance to show you what I can do," says the skinny guy.
"Okay... See that Giant Redwood over there?" says the head lumberjack. "Take your axe and chop it down."
The chap heads for the tree, and in five minutes he's knocking on the lumberjack's door. "I've cut that tree down," he says.
The lumberjack can't believe his eyes and says, "Where did you learn to chop down trees like that?" "In the Sahara Forest," says the puny man. "You mean the Sahara Desert?" says the lumberjack.
"Well, yes. That's what they call it now..."

Victoria: I got an anonymous letter.
David: Yeah? Who from?

What is E.T. short for?
Because he has little legs!

Fisherman: What are you fishing for, sonny?
Boy: I'm not fishing, I'm drowning worms!

Did you hear about the man who had BO on one side only?
He bought Right Guard, but couldn't find any Left Guard!

What do you call a wizard with a ladder?
Lord of the Rungs!

What's a Teenage TV soap set in Athens?
Dawson's Greek!

What kind of fish can't swim?
Dead ones!

What happened to the boy that slept with his head under his pillow?
The fairies stole all his teeth!

How do you know if there is an elephant in the pub?
Its bike is outside!

How do you know if there are two elephants in the pub?
There's a dent in the cross-bar!

How do you know if there are three elephants in the pub?
Stand on the bike and have a look in the window!

The owner of a large factory decided to make a surprise visit and check up on his staff. As he walked through the factory, he noticed a young man doing nothing but leaning against a post. He walked up to the young man and said angrily, "Just how much do you make in a week, Sonny?" "About 200 quid," replied the young man. Taking out a wad of £50 notes from his wallet, the owner counted out £800, slapped the money into the boy's hands and spat, "Here's a month's pay, now get out and don't come back!" Turning to one of the supervisors, he said, "I can't abide idleness! How long has that lazy so-and-so been working in my factory?" "He doesn't work here," said the supervisor,
"he was just delivering a pizza!"

What do whales eat?
Fish and ships!

Why did the man drag a cabbage on a lead?
He thought it was a collie!

What starts with "e," ends with "e" and only has one letter in it?
An envelope!

What do you get if you cross a herb and Doctor Who?
A thyme machine!

What do you get if you cross a gorilla and a prisoner?
A King Kongvict!

What should you give an elf who wants to be taller?
Elf raising flour!

What do you get if you cross a cake and a disco?
Abundance!

What do you get if you cross a giant ape and a self defence class?
Kong-fu!

A young boy was showing off to another, and he asked him if he knew what shape the world was. "I don't," said the second. "It's the same shape as the buttons on my jacket," said the first.
"Square," said the second.
"That's my Sunday jacket," said the first, "I meant my schoolday jacket. Now what shape is the world?"
"Square on Sundays, round on weekdays?" said the second boy.

Why did the man at the orange juice factory lose his job?
He couldn't concentrate!

What did the alien say to the garden?
Take me to your weeder!

What gets wetter the more it dries?
A towel!

What goes BUZZUB, BUZZUB?
A bee stuck to a yo-yo!

How do you communicate with a fish?
Drop him a line!

Where do sheep go to get haircuts?
To the Baa Baas!

What do sharks eat for pudding?
Jellyfish!

What do cats eat for breakfast?
Mice Crispies!

Who didn't invent the aeroplane?
The Wrong brothers!

Why do bagpipers walk when they play?
They're trying to get away from the noise!

How do you keep a skunk from smelling?
Hold his nose!

What looks like a horse and flies?
A flying horse!

Young Tyler was excited about his first day at school. So excited in fact, that only a few minutes after class started, he realised that he desperately needed to go to the bathroom. So, Tyler raised his hand politely to ask if he could be excused. Of course, the teacher said yes, but asked Tyler to be quick. Five minutes later Tyler returned, looking more desperate and embarrassed. "I can't find it," he admitted. The teacher sat Tyler down and drew him a little diagram to where he should go and asked him if he will be able to find it now. Tyler looked at the diagram, said "Yes" and went on his way.
Well, five minutes later he returned to the classroom and said to the teacher, "I can't find it." Frustrated, the teacher asked Tommy, a boy who has been at the school for a while, to help him find the bathroom. So, Tommy and Tyler went together and five minutes later they both returned and sit down at their seats. The teacher asked Tommy, "Well, did you find it?" Tommy said,
"Yes, he just had his boxer shorts on backwards."

English Teacher: Now, Jim. Can you give me a sentence using the word "fascinate"?
Jim: Yes. My raincoat has ten buttons but I can only fasten eight.

Two boll weevils grew up in Kent. One went to Hollywood and became a famous actor. The other stayed behind in the cabbage fields and never amounted to much.
The second one became known as the lesser of two weevils.

A man is sitting at home one night. Suddenly, there's a loud knock at the door. The man opens the door to find a six-foot beetle standing at the doorstep. "What in the world is this?" he asks. The beetle responds by attacking the man viciously, with a flurry of kicks and punches. Then the beetle leaves. The man crawls into his house and calls an ambulance. At the hospital, the nurse asks him how it happened. The guy tells her about the beetle and what happened. "Yes," the nurse says, with an understanding nod,
"there is a nasty bug going around at the moment..."

A clown goes into a restaurant.
"You can't come in here dressed like that!" says the manager.
"Oh go on, please!" says the clown, "I'm starving!"
"Alright," says the manager, "but don't try anything funny!"

What do you call a rock fan with a sausage on his face?
A headbanger!

What do you get if you cross a leopard and a bunch of flowers?
A beauty spot!

Two blokes are sitting in a pub. The first one says, "What's this thing they call a breathaliser?" The second bloke says, "It's a bag that tells you when you've drunk too much."
The first bloke says, "I married one of those years ago!"

A lady put a lonely hearts ad in the paper and had a reply which said, "I would love to meet you, but I have to tell you that I am eight feet tall, covered in green fur, with large fangs and slobbering lips. If you still want to meet me then I'll be under the clock at the Station at six o'clock next Saturday."
The lady replied,
"I would be interested in meeting you but please will you wear a red carnation and carry a copy of The New York Times so that I can recognise you?"

Did you hear about the monster who had an extra pair of hands?
No. Where did he keep them?
In a handbag!

Dad, I don't want to go to Australia!
Shut up and keep digging!

What do you call an underground train full of professors?
A tube of smarties!

Did you hear about the scientist who invented a glue that could stick anything to anything?
He can't get the lid off the bottle!

How do you stop a cockerel crowing on Sunday morning?
Have him for lunch on Saturday!

Did you hear about the drunk optician?
He made a spectacle of himself!

What's yellow and flickers?
A lemon with a loose connection somewhere!

This is a story about four people named Everybody, Somebody, Anybody and Nobody. There was an important job to be done and Everybody was sure that Somebody would do it.
Anybody could have done it, but Nobody did. Somebody got angry about this, because it was Everybody's job.
Everybody thought Anybody could do it, but Nobody realized that Everybody wouldn't do it.
It ended up that Everybody blamed Somebody when Nobody did what Anybody could have done!

How do you tell the weather with a piece of string?
Hang it up outside. If it moves, it's windy, if it gets wet, it's raining!

A salesman calls at a house.
"Madam," the salesman says,
"Can I interest you in a dishcloth, which comes with a free vacuum cleaner?"
"Gosh, that sounds like a bargain! How much for the cloth?"
"Seventy quid."

Why can't a bicycle stand on its own?
Because it's two-tyred!

Michael: I was on TV today.
Jeremy: You're kidding! How long were you on?
Michael: Five minutes. When my mum saw me she just told me to get off!

What do you get if you pour boiling water down a rabbit hole?
Hot cross bunnies!

Did you hear about the stupid photographer?
He saved dead lightbulbs to use in his darkroom!

The mafia boss found a stupid member of his gang sawing the legs off his bed.
"What are you doing that for?" demanded the boss.
"Just what you said, Boss," said the stupid thug.
"You told us to lie low for a bit!"

A mother marched her naughty little boy into the doctor's surgery.
"Doctor, is it possible that he could have taken his own tonsils out?" she asked.
"No," said the doctor.
"I told you so," said the mother. "Now, put them back!"

What starts with "t", ends with "t" and has "t" in it?
A teapot!

Arnold Schwarzenegger, Leonardo DiCaprio, and Tom Hanks were all making a movie about famous composers. Leo said, "I'd like to play Beethoven." Tom said, "I'd like to play Mozart."
Arnie said "I'll be Bach"!

Who went into the tiger's den and came out alive?
The tiger!

A man goes into a pharmacy and asks the assistant if she can give him something for hiccups. The assistant promptly reaches out and slaps the man's face. "What did you do that for?" the man asks. "Well, you don't have the hiccups anymore, do you?" said the assistant.
The man says, "No, but my wife does, she's outside in the car!"

What does Tim Henman fly to Mars in?
A Tennis Rocket!

How do you get an elephant on top of an oak tree?
Stand him on an acorn and wait 50 years!

What's big, grey and mutters?
A mumbo jumbo!

Where do sick boats go?
To the dock!

What do you get when you cross a car, a dog, and a bird?
A flying car-pet!

What's purple and needs help?
A damson in distress!

An elephant was drinking at a river one day, when he spotted a turtle asleep on a log. So, he ambled over and kicked it clear across the river.
"What did you do that for?" asked a passing giraffe.
"Because I recognised it as the exact same turtle that took a bite out of my trunk 53 years ago."
"Wow, what a memory!" said the giraffe.
"That's right," said the elephant, "I've got turtle recall!"

What do you get if you cross a skeleton, a feather and a joke book?
Rib ticklers!

Bill: How does your head feel today?
Ben: As good as new.
Bill: It should be as good as new - it's never been used!

A panicked passenger on the Titanic: Captain, How far away is the nearest land?
Captain: Two miles, Sir.
Passenger: Thank heavens! In which direction?
Captain: Downwards!

What is invisible and smells like carrots?
Bunny Farts!

What runs but can't walk?
A tap!

Why did the little biscuit cry?
Because his mum was a wafer so long!

If a crocodile makes shoes, what does a banana make?
Slippers!

What kind of bed does a mermaid sleep in?
A water bed!

A mean cowboy went into a saddler's shop and asked for one spur.
"One spur?" asked the saddler. "Surely you mean a pair of spurs, sir?"
"No, just one," replied the cowboy.
"If I can get one side of the horse to go, the other side is bound to come with it!"

If two's company and three's a crowd, what's four and five?
Nine!

How can you tell if two octopi are dating?
They walk arm in arm in arm in arm!

What does an octopus wear in winter?
A coat of arms!

Three burglars are running away from the scene of a crime, being chased by the police. They turn a corner and see some empty sacks lying on the floor and decide to hide in them. When the police catch up they see the sacks and are very suspicious. They kick the first sack and hear "Meow! Meow!" and think there's a cat inside. They then kick the second sack and hear "Woof! Woof!" and think there's a dog inside. They then kick the third sack and hear:
"Potato! Potato!"

What do you get if you cross a mouse and a bottle of olive oil?
A squeak that oils itself!

What do you get if you cross a bunch of flowers with a burglar?
Robbery with violets!

A woman is thinking about buying a mink coat.
"Will it be all right in the rain?" she asked the shop assistant.
"Have you ever seen a mink with an umbrella?" he said.

A man told his doctor that he wasn't able to do all the things around the house that he used to do. When the examination was complete, he said,
"Now, Doc. I can take it. Tell me in plain English what is wrong with me."
"Well, in plain English," the doctor replied, "you're just very lazy."
"Okay," said the man. "Now give me the medical term so I can tell my wife."

Why did Silly Sue throw her guitar away?
Because it had a hole in the middle.

What became of the man who was swallowed by a cow?
He became the man in the moo!

A man hears a knock at his door. He opens the door, looks around, then down, and sees a snail on his step. He picks it up, and throws it into the street. Ten years later, the man hears a knock at his door. When he opens the door, there sits the same snail. The snail says,
"Oi! What was that all about?!"

How do you get an elephant into the fridge?
1. Open door.
2. Insert elephant.
3. Close door.

How do you get a giraffe into the fridge?
1. Open door.
2. Remove elephant.
3. Insert giraffe.
4. Close door.

The lion, the king of the jungle, decided to have a party. He invited all the animals in the jungle, and they all came except one. Which one?
The giraffe, because he was still in the fridge!

What happened to the witch with an upside-down nose?
Every time she sneezed her hat blew off!

Why did the boy bring toilet paper to the birthday party?
Because he's a party pooper!

What happened when 500 hares got loose on the main street?
The police had to comb the area!

A little boy ran home from school on the first day and pestered his mother into taking him into a toy shop. When they got there he insisted that she buy him a gun. "But why do you need a gun?" asked his mother.
"Because teacher told us she was going to teach us to draw tomorrow!"

"Farmer Giles, why do you have two barrels on your shotgun?" "So that if I miss the fox with the first I can get him with the other."
"Why not fire with the other one first, then?"

Two men were out hunting when one of them saw a rabbit. "Quick," said the first, "shoot it!" "I can't," said the second. "My gun isn't loaded."
"Well," said the first, "you know that, and I know that, but the rabbit doesn't!"

What yells and jumps from cake to cake?
Tarzipan!

God is talking to one of his angels. He says, "I've just created a 24-hour period of alternating light and darkness on Earth."
The angel says, "What are you going to do now?"
God says, "I'm going to call it a day!"

Does your mum like shopping on the Internet?
No, the trolley keeps rolling off the computer!

What do you call a fish without an eye?
Fsh!

"Can I have some two-handed cheese, please?" a man in a restaurant asked the waiter.
"What do you mean, 'two-handed cheese'?" asked the waiter.
"You know, the kind you eat with one hand and hold your nose with the other."

How can you cut the sea in two?
With a seasaw!

Does she have something on her mind?
Only if she's got a hat on.

First Woman: Whenever I'm down in the dumps I buy myself a new hat.
Second Woman: Oh, so that's where you get them!

Father: Gosh, your history teacher was there when I went to school!
Bobby: He's very old. He's got so many wrinkles he has to screw his hat on!

What does a boy monster do when a girl monster rolls her eyes at him?
He picks them up and rolls them back!

What's green and points north?
A magnetic gherkin!

Who invented the kangaroo?
A man with a tin factory and lots of garoos!

Did you hear about the karate champion who joined the army?
Every time he saluted, he nearly killed himself!

What do you call a hippy's wife?
Mississippi!

What do you call a scared wicked old woman who lives by the sea?
A chicken sandwitch!

What's in the middle of a jellyfish?
His jellybutton!

Why did the ram run over the cliff?
He didn't see the ewe turn!

Where was King Solomon's temple?
On his forehead!

A police officer was escorting a prisoner to jail when his hat blew off.
"Shall I run and get it for you?" asked the prisoner obligingly.
"You must think I'm stupid," said the officer.
"You wait here and I'll get it!"

What's wet and wiggly and says "How do you do?" sixteen times?
Two octopi shaking hands!

Why did the girl have her hair in a bun?
Because she had her nose in a hamburger!

Where do mermaids go to see movies?
The dive-in!

What do you get if you cross a book and a pound of fat?
Lard of the rings!

What do you get if you cross a skunk and a pair of tennis rackets?
Ping pong!

What's the best way to make a pair of trousers last?
Make the coat first!

What does Harry Potter ask for when he arrives at a hotel?
Broom service!

Why was Cinderella such a bad football player?
Her coach was a pumpkin!

Two guys are walking in the desert; one is carrying a lamp post, the other one has a telephone booth.
"Why are you carrying a telephone booth?" says the first. "When the lions come, I put it down, climb into it and I'll be safe," said the second. "Why are you carrying a lamp post?"
"So that when the lions come, I can throw it away and I can run faster."

Waiter: How many people for lunch?
Cannibal: Two each, please.

How do really small people call each other?
On microphones!

How did the carpenter break his teeth?
He chewed his nails!

A red house is made out of red bricks, a yellow house of yellow bricks, so what is a green house made from?
Glass!

Teacher: Hey! You can't sleep in my class!
Student: I could if you didn't talk so loud!

How do you get an elephant out of a tree?
Stand it on a leaf and wait until Autumn!

What do you call a cow who has just given birth?
Decalf-inated!

What do tall monarchs wear?
High-king boots!

"Doctor, will this ointment clear up my itchy spots?"
"I'm not making any rash promises!"

What kind of elephants live at the North Pole?
Cold ones!

Little Johnny's mother took him with her to the bank on a busy Friday. They were in the queue behind a rather large lady wearing a business suit, complete with a mobile phone in her hand. As the mother patiently waited, Little Johnny looked at the woman in front of him and observed loudly,
"Hey, Mum, she's REALLY FAT!"
The lady looked at Johnny, made eye contact with his mother and gave an understanding smile. His Mum smiled back sheepishly.
After a minute or two, Johnny spread his hands as far as they would go and loudly said, "Her bum is THIS BIG!" At this, the lady glared at Johnny. His embarrassed mother told him off. Again after a couple of minutes Johnny said loudly,
"Look how the fat hangs over her belt!"
The lady turned and told Johnny's mother to control her rude child and his mother threatened him with a good spanking. The lady got to the front of the line when her phone started beeping and Johnny shouted at the top of his voice,
"LOOK OUT MUM, SHE'S REVERSING!"

Why did the fish blush?
Because it saw the ocean's bottom!

What do you get if you cross a bottle of washing up liquid and a mouse?
Bubble and squeak!

What do you call a squad of flying rabbits?
The hare force!

Waiter, this stew isn't fit for a pig to eat!
I'm terribly sorry, Sir. I'll bring you something that is...

How do you show your appreciation for Father Christmas?
Santapplause!

The policeman couldn't believe his eyes as he saw the woman drive past him, busily knitting. Quickly he pulled alongside the vehicle, wound down his window and shouted, "Pull over!"
"No," she replied, "socks!"

What do you get if you cross a flock of sheep and a radiator?
Central bleating!

How do Welsh people eat cheese?
Caerphilly!

What's brown and sticky?
A stick!

Did you hear about the snooker-mad monster? He went to the doctor because he didn't feel well.
"What do you eat?" asked the doctor.
"For breakfast I have a couple of red snooker balls, and at lunchtime I grab a black, a pink and two yellows. I have a brown with my tea in the afternoon, and then a blue and another pink for dinner."
"I know why you are not feeling well," exclaimed the doctor.
"You're not getting enough greens!"

Patient: Doctor, my hair keeps falling out in clumps, can you give me anything to keep it in?
Doctor: Certainly, here's a paper bag!

What's white and fluffy and beats its chest?
A meringue-utan!

"Doctor, some days I feel like a tee-pee and other days I feel like a wig-wam."
"I see, you're two tents!"

What happened to the man that opened a newspaper shop?
It blew away!

So, there was this little potato and her mum and dad sitting at home one evening eating dinner. The little potato said, "Mum? Dad? I have some really big news! I'm going to marry John Motson!" Mum Potato sighed and looked very sad,
"Oh dear, love. We didn't want you to marry a common tater!"

What do you get when you cross a giraffe and a rooster?
An animal that wakes up people on the top floor!

Customer: How much is that duck?
Shopkeeper: Ten pounds.
Customer: Okay, could you please send me the bill?
Shopkeeper: I'm sorry, but you'll have to take the whole bird!

What do people do in clock factories?
They make faces all day!

What do you call two rows of cabbages?
A dual cabbageway!

Why did the chicken cross the playground?
To get to the other slide!

What goes ho-ho whoosh, ho-ho whoosh?
Santa caught in a revolving door!

What colour is a hiccup?
Burple!

How do elves get indigestion?
By goblin their dinner!

What's brown, white and yellow and travels at 100 miles an hour?
A train driver's egg sandwich!

Why did the bees go on strike?
For more honey and shorter flowers!

What keeps jazz musicians on earth?
Groovity!

"Waiter, there's a hand in my soup."
"That's not your soup, sir, that's your finger bowl."

Who is the biggest gangster in the sea?
Al Caprawn!

What do you get if you cross a dog with a game of football?
Spot the ball!

What are baby witches called?
Hallowe'enies!

How do eels get around the seabed?
They go by octobus!

What's grey and squirts jam at you?
A mouse eating a doughnut!

Who earns a living by driving his customers away?
A cab driver!

Why did the cat want to be a nurse?
She wanted to be a first-aid kit!

There once was a lady who had identical twin boys, whom she named Amal and Juan. Unfortunately she could not look after them so she had to give them up for adoption. One couple adopted Juan and moved to Spain. Another couple adopted Amal and moved to Australia. Ten years later Juan sent his birth mother a letter and a picture of himself. The mother told her husband she wished Amal would send her a picture too. The husband said,
"What's the point? When you've seen Juan, you've seen Amal!"

What do you get when you cross a cheetah and a pizza?
Fast food!

How can you use the colours green, pink, and yellow in a sentence?
When the phone goes "green! green!" You "pink" it up and say "yellow!"

What happened when the tramp stole a bottle of perfume?
He was arrested for fragrancy!

Where do people go dancing in California?
San Frandisco!

A fishmonger is 6 feet tall, wears size 34 trousers and size 12 shoes. What does he weigh?
Fish!

What do you call a lion who has eaten your mother's sister?
An aunt-eater!

What do you get if you cross a student and an alien?
Something from another university!

Did you hear about the village idiot buying bird seed?
He said he wanted to grow some birds!

If a dictionary goes from A to Z, what goes from Z to A?
A zebra!

Did you hear about the girl who wasn't pretty and wasn't ugly?
She was pretty ugly!

What do you get if you cross a bee with a quarter of a pound of ground beef?
A humburger!

No. Billy, you can't play with the hammer. You'll hurt your fingers.
No, I won't, Dad. Sis is going to hold the nails for me!

A scuba diver was 20 feet down under the water and saw a man without any breathing equipment at all. The man without the gear went down 20 more feet and the man with the scuba gear followed him. He kept following until they reached the sea bed.
Now the man with the gear is confused, so he takes a waterproof chalk and board out of his bag and writes:
"How do you stay down here without any gear?" The man without the gear takes the chalk and writes:
"I'm drowning, you idiot!"

Bob: I was on the telly last night.
Rob: Really?!
Bob: Yes, when I'm drunk I'll sleep anywhere!

What do you get if you dial 666?
Upside-down policemen!

Why do ducks watch the news?
To get the feather forecast!

When is the vet busiest?
When it's raining cats and dogs!

What do you give a pig with a sore throat?
Oinkment!

What did the duck say when he'd finished shopping?
Put it on my bill please!

Which month has 28 days?
All of them!

Why are giraffes so slow to apologise?
It takes them a really long time to swallow their pride!

Did you hear about the boxing match between the hedgehog and the badger?
The hedgehog won on points!

What is white when it's dirty and black when it's clean?
A blackboard!

What's green, red and yellow and wears boxing gloves?
Fruit punch!

What animal would you like to be on a cold day?
A little otter!

What did the bra say to the hat?
You go on ahead while I give these two a lift!

Why is tennis such a loud game?
Because each player raises a racquet!

Three pieces of string went to a restaurant to eat. The first string went in and the waiter looked at him and said, "Are you a string?" and the string said, "Yes." So the waiter said, "I'm sorry. We don't serve strings." The second string came in and the waiter looked at him and said, "Are you a string?" and the string said, "Yes." So the waiter said, "I'm sorry. We don't serve strings." Then the third string tied himself in a bundle and messed up his ends to look untidy. He walked into the restaurant and the waiter looked him up and down and said, "Are you a string?" and the string said,
"No, I'm a frayed knot!"

What do you get if you cross a pudding and a skunk?
A smelly jelly!

What do you get if you cross an alligator and King Midas?
A croc of gold!

What's green and loud?
A froghorn!

What is at the end of everything?
The letter G!

What do mermaids have on toast?
Mermerlade!

Why do elephants never forget?
Because nobody ever tells them anything!

Teacher: That's the stupidest boy in the whole school.
Mother: That's my son.
Teacher: Oh! I'm so sorry.
Mother: You're sorry?

Two babies were sat in their prams, when one baby shouted to the other, "Are you a girl or a boy?" "I don't know," replied the other baby. "What do you mean, you don't know?" said the first baby. "I mean I don't know how to tell the difference!" was the reply. "Well, I do," said the first baby. "I'll climb into your pram and find out." He carefully climbed into the other baby's pram and disappeared beneath the blankets. After a minute, he came out with a big smile on his face. "You're a little girl, and I'm a little boy," he said proudly. "You're ever so clever," said the baby girl, "but how can you tell?" "It's easy really," said the boy.
"You've got pink booties and I've got blue ones."

What do you get if you cross a detective with a cat?
A peeping Tom!

Patient: Doctor, I snore so loudly I keep myself awake!
Doctor: Sleep in another room then.

Did you hear about the cannibal policeman who was arrested?
He was caught grilling his suspects!

What did one eye say to the other?
Between you and me, something smells!

How did the barber win the marathon?
He took a short cut!

Why was night cricket invented?
Because bats like to sleep in the daytime!

What do you get if you cross a singer and a tall ladder?
Someone who can easily get the high notes!

What's yellow on the inside and green on the outside?
A banana spy in cucumberland!

What have Batman and burglars got in common?
They never go out without robbin'!

What do you get if you cross a monster and a chicken?
Free strange eggs!

What did the big chimney say to the small chimney?
You're too little to smoke!

Who carries a basket, visits Grandma and steals her jewellery?
Little Red Robin Hood!

What kind of dog tells time?
A watch dog!

Where do electric eggs come from?
A battery hen!

What do you get if you cross a frog with a traffic warden?
Toad away!

How do you kill a circus?
Go straight for the juggler!

What do you get if you cross a snake with a building site?
A boa-constructor!

A boastful American from Texas was being shown the sights of London by a taxi-driver.
"What's that building over there Mr Cab Driver?" asked the Texan.
"That's the Tower of London, sir," replied the taxi-driver.
"Say, in Texas we can put up buildings like that in two weeks," said the Texan.
A little while later he said,
"And what's that building we're passing now, Cabbie?"
"That's Buckingham Palace, sir. Where the Queen lives."
"Is that so?" said the Texan. "Do you know back in Texas we could put a place like that up in a week?"
A few minutes later they were passing Westminster Abbey.
The American asked again,
"Hey, Cabbie, what's that building over there?"
"I'm afraid I don't know, sir," replied the taxi-driver.
"It wasn't there this morning."

What did the big flower say to the little flower?
Hey, Bud!

What do you get when you cross an octopus and a cow?
An animal that can milk itself!

A fire started on a farm. The fire department were called to put it out, but they were out on a call. Someone suggested that the nearby volunteers should be called. The volunteers arrived in a knackered old fire engine. They raced straight towards the fire and parked right in the middle of the flames. The firemen jumped off and frantically started spraying water in all directions. Soon they had the blaze under control. The farmer was so impressed with the volunteer firemens' work and was so grateful that his farm had been spared, that he gave the volunteers £1,000. A local news reporter asked the volunteer fire captain what the department planned to do with the funds. He said,
"The first thing we're going do is get the brakes fixed on the fire engine."

A farmer was showing a schoolboy from town round his farm when they came to a field where the farmer's flock of sheep was grazing.
"How many sheep do you reckon there are?" the farmer asked proudly.
"Seven hundred and sixty-four," replied the boy after a few seconds.
The farmer gaped. "That's exactly right, boy. How did you count them so quickly?"
"Simple," said the boy genius. "I just counted the legs and divided by four!"

What's grey and goes boom, boom, boom?
An elephant skipping!

Where do pigs buy things?
Pork shops!

How do you find rice and pasta on the Internet?
Use a starch engine!

What does a vicar use to surf the Internet?
A church mouse!

What's Tarzan's favourite carol?
Jungle bells!

What animals use nutcrackers?
Toothless squirrels!

What is an hedgehog's favourite food?
Prickled onions!

What's round, white and giggles?
A tickled onion!

What do you call a fly with no wings?
A walk!

Why did Harry Potter get a sun roof?
He wanted a broom with a view!

Why did the stupid racing car driver make ten pit stops during the Grand Prix?
He was asking for directions!

Boat attendant: Come in number 9, your time is up!
Assistant: But sir, we have only 8 rowing boats.
Boat attendant: Oh dear... Are you in trouble, number 6?

A man was driving down the highway and he was pulled over by a policeman. The policeman said, "You were driving 85 miles per hour." "How can you possibly say that?" the man said.
"I've only been out for 20 minutes!"

What has four legs and flies?
Two pairs of trousers!

What do you get if you cross a pig and a box of itching powder?
Pork scratchings!

Why is a slippery pavement like music?
If you don't C sharp, you'll B flat!

What kind of umbrella does a Russian carry when it's raining?
A wet one!

What do you get if you cross an elephant and a bottle of whisky?
Trunk and disorderly!

How do you send a message in the forest?
By moss code!

Have you heard the joke about the dump?
Don't worry, it's a load of rubbish!

What do ghosts take for bad colds?
Coffin drops!

How does a tennis player sneeze?
A-tennis-shoe! A-tennis-shoe!

Why do bees have sticky hair?
Because they have honeycombs!

A lady answers the door to a young man in overalls. "Can I help you?" she says. "Yes, I am a handyman,.and I was wondering if you needed any work done around your house," said the youngster. "As a matter of fact I do, I need my porch painted. How much will you charge?" the lady asked. "How about £20?" the lad said. "Okay. The paint, ladders, and everything else that you will need are in the shed," said the lady. About 30 minutes later, the young man went up to the house. "Done already?" the lady asked. "Yes, it's now a lovely bright blue and I had some extra paint, so I put two coats on," the lad replied. "Great!" the lady said, and handed him the £20. The lad was walking to his bicycle when he turned around and said,
"Oh, and by the way, it's a Ferrari, not a Porsche."

What do you get when you cross a old lady and an octopus?
I don't know, but it's really good at Bingo!

How do you get out of an all brick room with only a mirror and a table?
You look in the mirror, you see what you saw, you take the saw and cut the table in half. Two halves make a whole and you climb through it!

What do you call a surgeon with eight arms?
A doctorpus!

What do you get when you cross a frog and a rabbit?
A rabbit that says "ribbit"!

Why aren't elephants allowed on beaches?
They can't keep their trunks up!

What do you call the part of a pig in a film?
A ham roll!

Did you hear about the bloke that drowned in his bowl of muesli?
A strong currant pulled him under!

What's better than a drip dry vampire?
A wash and werewolf!

A guy driving a Nissan Micra pulled up to a traffic light next to a Rolls-Royce. He rolled down his window and shouted to the driver of the Rolls, "Hey, that's a nice car. You got a phone in your Rolls? I've got a phone in my Micra!" The driver of the Rolls looked over and said snobbishly, "Yes, I have a phone." The driver of the Micra said, "That's great! Hey, you got a TV in there? You know, I got a TV in the back of my Micra!" The driver of the Rolls, quite irritated by now, replied, "Of course I have a television. A Roll-Royce is the finest luxury car in the world!"

The driver of the Micra said, "Have you got a bed in there? I got a bed in the back of my Micra!" The driver of the Rolls, upset that he did not have a bed, drove away and went straight to the dealer, where he promptly ordered a bed to be installed in the back of his Rolls-Royce. The next morning, he returned to pick up his car, and the bed looked superb. It came complete with silk sheets and a brass-trimmed headboard. It was clearly a bed fit for a Rolls-Royce. So the driver of the Rolls began searching for the Nissan Micra. He drove around all day and finally found it late that night. It was parked, with all the windows fogged up from the inside. He got out and knocked on the window. When there wasn't any answer, he continued knocking and knocking until eventually, the owner of the Micra lowered the window, and stuck his soaking wet head out.

"I now have a bed in the back of my Rolls-Royce," the driver of the Rolls stated arrogantly.

The Micra driver looked at him and said, "You got me out of the bath to tell me that?!"

A customer at Tony's grocer's asked him one day:
"Tony, what makes you so clever?"
"Well, I wouldn't share my secret with just anyone," Tony says, "but since you're a good customer, I'll tell you... Fish heads. If you eat enough of them, you'll be as clever as I am in no time."
"Wow, do you sell them in here?" the customer asks.
"I sure do, only £4 each," says Tony.
The customer buys three.
A week later, he's back in the store complaining that the fish heads were disgusting and he isn't any cleverer.
"You didn't eat enough!" says Tony. The customer goes home with 20 more fish heads. Two weeks later, he's back and this time he's really angry.
"Hey, Tony," he says, "you're selling me fish heads for £4 each when I just found out I can buy the whole fish for £2! You're ripping me off!"
"You see?" says Tony. "You're cleverer already!"

Who was bigger, Mr Bigger or his son?
His son...he was a little Bigger!

What is H204?
Drinking!

What do you call a funny bloke whose face changes colours?
A stand-up chameleon!

Did you hear about the bloke who set up a flea circus?
He started it from scratch!

What's black and white and red all over?
An exploding zebra!

One day a little girl was watching her mum make a roast beef. The mother cut off the ends, wrapped it in string, and put it in a roasting tin. The little girl asked her mum why she cut off the ends of the roast beef.
Mum said: "Because that's how Granny always does it." That night Granny came to dinner and the little girl and her mum went to her and asked why she cut the ends off a roast beef before cooking.
Granny replied, "Because that's how Great Granny always does it."
Now Great Granny was quite old and in a nursing home. But the little girl went with her mum and Granny to see her and ask why she cuts the ends off her roast beef. She looked at them and said:
"So it will fit in the pan, of course!"

What do you give an injured lemon?
Lemonade!

What do you call a country where everybody has a pink car?
A pink carnation!

Doctor, everyone keeps ignoring me...
Next please!

Bob: Did you know that the coolest person on Earth has gone deaf?
Rob: Really, who's that?
Bob: What?!

What does an axe murderer do with a pen and paper?
Writes his chopping list!

What did the mouse say when his friend broke a tooth?
Hard cheese!

What do you get when you put a fish and an elephant together?
Swimming trunks!

Why did the basketball floor get wet?
The players dribbled on it!

Why did the lady miss her husband?
Because she never shot a gun before!

How do pop stars stay cool?
Sit next to their fans!

What's a posthumous work?
Something written by someone after they've died!

Why isn't whispering permitted in class?
Because it's not aloud!

Where do birds meet for coffee?
In a nest-café!

Read all about it!

Some of the right writers for the job...

The Luggage Thief by Amy Suitcase
DIY Tips by Andy Mann
Medical Dictionary by Ivan Orfulkoff
Evening Casseroles by Stuart Nine
Long Division by Carry One
Wigwam Living by T. P. Dwella
You Can't be Serious by R. U. Kidden
Camping Out by Guy Rope
Truck Rental by Lisa Lorry
Gymnastics by Ben D. Body
Jungle Survival by Lionel Getcha
The World of Sweets by Penny Choo
Delicious Cakes by Sue Neaten
Investing in France by Frank Cinderbank
Home Plumbing by Walter Evriware
My Hard Life by Ida Tuftime
100 Ways with Eggs by E. Titror
Travels Down Under by Sidney Ticket
Caring for Your Cat by May Kitpur
Friendly Neighbours by Len Dahand

What nationality is Santa Claus?
North Polish!

Who was the toughest cowboy 65 million years ago?
Tyrannosaurus Tex!

What's the quietest place in the world?
The complaints department at the parachute factory!

Waiter, you have your thumb on my steak!
I know sir, I don't want it to fall on the floor again!

What do you carry almonds in?
A nut case!

An enthusiastic door-to-door vacuum cleaner salesman goes to the first house in his new patch. He knocks, a lady opens the door, and before she has a chance to say anything, he runs inside and dumps horse manure all over the carpet.
He says, "Madam, if this vacuum cleaner doesn't pick all this up, I'll eat every chunk of it."
She turns to him and says, "Do you want ketchup on that?"
The salesman says, "Why?"
She says, "We just moved in and we haven't got the electricity turned on yet."

What goes "Ha, ha, ha, plop"?
A man laughing his head off!

What's the best way to keep water out of your house?
Don't pay the water rates!

A woman is having a baby and she faints clean away as she's giving birth. She comes round later and asks the nearest doctor about her baby.
"You had twins, a boy and a girl, and they are both fine and healthy," says the doctor. "Luckily, your brother was here and he named them both for you."
"Oh no, not my brother! He's an idiot! What did he call the girl?"
"Denise," the doctor replies.
"Oh, that's not so bad," she says, "and what did he call the boy?"
The doctor answers, "Denephew."

Girl: Mom, mom a monster's just bitten my foot off!
Mom: Well keep out of the kitchen, I've just washed the floor.

A girl called her friend and said, "Please come over and help me, I have this really difficult jigsaw puzzle, and I can't work out how to start it." The friend asked, "What is it a puzzle of?" The girl said, "From the picture on the box, I guess it's a tiger." The friend heads on over to the girl's house. The girl lets her friend in the door and shows her where she has the puzzle spread all over the table. The friend looks at the pieces for a moment, then the box, and then the pieces again. She turns to the girl and says, "First, no matter what I do, I'm not going to be able to show you how to make these pieces look like that tiger. Second, I think you should relax, have a cup of tea, and put all the Frosties back in the box."

The little old lady seated herself right behind the coach driver on a long trip. Every ten minutes or so she'd pipe up, "Have we reached Newton Blarney yet, sonny?" "No, Madam not yet. I'll let you know," he replied, time after time. The hours passed, the old woman kept asking for Newton Blarney again and again and again, and finally the village came into view. Sighing with relief, the driver slammed on the brakes, pulled the coach over and called out, "This is where you get out, Madam!" "Is this Newton Blarney?" "Yes!" he bellowed. "Get out!" "Oh, I'm going all the way to Edinburgh, sonny," she explained. "It's just that my daughter told me that when we got this far, I should eat my sandwiches."

What did the blanket say to the bed?
Don't worry, I've got you covered!

What did the metric alien say?
Take me to your litre!

What's green, hairy and takes Aspirin?
A gooseberry with a hangover!

A man comes out of a shopping mall to find that the side of his parked car is rammed in. Seeing a note under the windscreen wipers, he read it. On the paper is written:
"As I'm writing this, about a dozen people are watching me. They think I'm giving you my name, phone number, and the details of my insurance company. But I'm not."

Why did the dinosaur cross the road?
Because chickens weren't invented!

A man enters a barber shop for a shave. While the barber is foaming him up, he mentions the problem he has getting a close shave around his cheeks.
"I have just the thing," says the barber, taking a small wooden ball from a nearby drawer. "Just place this between your cheek and gum."
The client places the ball in his mouth and the barber starts to give him the closest shave he has ever had.
After a few strokes, the client asks: "What if I swallow this ball?"
"No problem," says the barber, "just bring it back tomorrow, like everyone else does!"

What do you call dirty pasta?
Muckaroni!

What happened when the cannibals ate a comedian?
They had a feast of fun!

A policeman pulls a car over on a lonely back road and approaches the lady driver. "Madam, is there a reason that you're weaving all over the road?"
The woman replied, "Oh officer, thank goodness you're here! I almost had an accident! I looked up and there was a tree right in front of me. I swerved to the left and there was another tree in front of me. I swerved to the right and there was another tree in front of me!"
Reaching through the side window to the rear view mirror, the officer replied, "That's your air freshener."

What's the difference between a gorilla and a grape?
They're both purple, except for the gorilla!

Why is Cinderella rubbish at cricket?
Because she keeps running away from the ball!

How much did the American pirate pay for his earrings?
A buccaneer!

Why did the picture go to jail?
Because it was framed!

What does a dentist call his x-rays?
Tooth-pics!

What has a bottom at the top?
I don't know.
Your legs!

What do you get if you cross a bear with a freezer?
A teddy brrrrr!

What happens if you eat the Christmas decorations?
You get tinselitus!

Fred: I was top of the class last week.
Mum: How did you manage that?
Fred: I managed to answer a question about elephants. The teacher asked us how many legs an elephant had, and I said five.
Mum: But that's not right.
Fred: I know, but I was the nearest!

"May I have another slice of lemon?" a man asked the barmaid.
"We don't have any lemons," said the barmaid.
"Oops!" said the man. "Then I've just squeezed your canary into my gin and tonic!"

Why do so few dogs visit psychiatrists?
Because they're not allowed on the couch!

What do you get if you cross a skeleton and a dog?
An animal that buries itself in the garden!

What do you get if you cross teeth with candy?
Dental floss!

What eats bananas at a thousand miles an hour?
King Kongcorde!

What did Tarzan say to his wife?
Jane, it's a jungle out there!

After a young couple brought their new baby home, the wife suggested that her husband should try his hand at changing nappies. "I'm busy," he said, "I'll do the next one." The next time came around and she asked again. The husband looked at his wife.
"I didn't mean the next nappy. I meant the next baby."

How did Harry Potter use magic on his driving test?
He turned into a petrol station!

Teacher: You're late for school again!
Billy: Yes, I'm sorry, sir. I overslept.
Teacher: I thought I told you to get an alarm clock!
Billy: I did, sir, but there are nine of us in our family.
Teacher: What on earth has that got to do with it?
Billy: The alarm was only set for eight!

What game do cannibals play at parties?
Swallow my leader!

What goes tick, tick, woof, woof?
A watch dog!

What's sweet and sour and hard?
Kung-food!

Three pigs went into a bar. The first pig ordered one beer and asked the barman, "Where's the loo?" The barman said, "Down the corridor to the right." The second pig ordered two beers and asked the bartender, "Where's the loo?" "Down the corridor to the right," said the barman. The third pig ordered three beers and asked for the bill. The barman said, "Don't you want to go to the loo?"
"No," said the pig, "I'm the pig that goes wee wee wee all the way home!"

How do you get six donkeys in a fire engine?
Two in the front, two on the back and two on the top going "Heehaw Heehaw Heehaw"!

What is the best thing to take into the desert?
A thirst aid kit!

Bill, Jim, and Scott were at a business convention together and were sharing a large suite on the top of a 75-storey hotel. After a long day of meetings they were shocked to hear that the lifts in their hotel were out of order and they would have to climb 75 flights of stairs to get to their room. Bill said to Jim and Scott, "Let's break the boredom of the climb by concentrating on something interesting. I'll tell jokes for 25 flights, and Jim can sing songs for 25 flights, and Scott can tell sad stories the rest of the way!" At the 26th floor, Bill stopped telling jokes and Jim began to sing. At the 51st floor, Jim stopped singing and Scott began to tell sad stories.
"I will tell my saddest story first," he said. "I've left the room key in the car!"

What do you get if you cross a skunk and a pair of rubber boots?
Smelly wellies!

What happens when it rains cats and dogs?
You step in a poodle!

What do you call a bloke who's always there when you need him?
Andy!

How does Santa Claus take photos?
With his North Pole-aroid camera!

Why did the man put his money in the freezer?
He wanted cold hard cash!

How do you get Pikachu on a bus?
You Pok'imon!

There were three idiots on a roof, a big idiot, a medium idiot and a short idiot. The big and the medium idiots fell off. Why didn't the short one?
Because he was a little moron!

A little old lady was at home when the telephone rang. She answered it and the voice on the other end said: "I am The Viper and I'm three streets away!" The little old lady thought it was just children playing and put down the phone. Half an hour later the phone rang again. The lady answered it and the voice said: "I am The Viper and I'm two streets away!" She started to get a little scared. A few minutes later the phone rang again. She answered it and the voice said: "I am The Viper and I'm one street away!" Now she was really scared. A few minutes later the doorbell rang! She took her husband's walking stick and rushed to the door. She opened it and waved the stick out of the door. The voice said:
"I am The Viper! I have come to clean your Vindows!"

What's the difference between Tony Blair and a dog?
Tony Blair usually wears a suit– a dog just pants!

When does five and five make eleven?
When you're stupid!

What did Pooh say to his agent?
Show me the honey!

Light Bulb Jokes

How many rude people does it take to change a light bulb?
None of your business, Nosey!

How many psychiatrists does it take to change a light bulb?
Only one, but the bulb has got to really want to change!

How many Real Men does it take to change a light bulb?
None: Real Men aren't afraid of the dark!

How many Boy Bands does it take to change a light bulb?
Nobody knows. Boy Bands don't last as long as light bulbs!

How many jugglers does it take to change a light bulb?
One, but it takes at least three light bulbs!

How many hairdressers does it take to change a light bulb?
Five. One to change it and the other four to stand around saying, "That looks really lovely, Mandy!"

How many Mafia hitmen does it take to change a light bulb?
Three. One to change the light bulb, one to be a witness, and the third to shoot the witness!

How many Blue Peter presenters does it take to change a light bulb?
Two. One to change it, and one to turn the old one into an attractive Christmas tree decoration.

How many secret agents does it take to change a light bulb?
Shh!

How many footballers does it take to change a light bulb?
Nine. One to change it and eight to jump on him and smother him with kisses!

How many Elvis Presleys does it take to change a light bulb?
Four: One for the money, two for the show, three to get ready, and four to go!

Light Bulb Jokes continued

How many magicians does it take to change a light bulb?
It depends on what you want to change it into!

How many pessimists does it take to change a light bulb?
What's the point? It'll only blow again!

How many maths students does it take to change a light bulb?
I dunno, I forgot my calculator!

How many monkeys does it take to change a light bulb?
Two. One to change it and one to scratch his bum!

How many SAS men does it take to change a light bulb?
Three. One to change it and two to shout "GO! GO! GO!"

How many teenage girls does it take to change a light bulb?
Four. One to change it and three to hear all about it on the phone afterwards!

How many vampires does it take to change a light bulb?
None, they like it in the dark!

How many cops does it take to screw in a light bulb?
None. It turned itself in!

How many owls does it take to change a light bulb?
T'woo!

A man was sitting in a chair in his house when the heavy rain started a flood. An hour later a rescue boat came and the people in it shouted to him, "Come on, get in!" The man said, "No, I have faith in God...he'll save me!" so the boat left. Two hours later he was forced to move to the upstairs floor. Another rescue boat came and said, "Come on, get in!" Again the man said, "No, I have faith in God...he'll save me!" Three hours later he was forced to move up onto the roof. A helicopter came and the pilot said, "Come on, get in!" Again the man said, "No, I have faith in God...he'll save me." An hour later the flood water rose over his head and the man drowned... He arrived in heaven and he asked St Peter why God didn't save him. St. Peter said,
"You're joking! He sent you two rescue boats and a helicopter!"

What do you call an overweight alien?
An extra cholesterol!

A tramp asks a man for two pounds. The man asked, "Will you buy alcohol?" The tramp said, "No." The man asked, "Will you gamble it away?" The tramp said, "No."
Then the man asked, "Will you come home with me so my wife can see what happens to a man who doesn't drink or gamble?"

What's a sheep's favourite holiday destination?
The Baaahaaamaaas!

Bob was in a terrible accident at work and ripped off both of his ears. Since he was permanently scarred, he settled with his employers for a huge sum of money and went on his way.
He invested his money in a small, but growing telecom business. After signing on the dotted line, he realised that he knew nothing about running such a business and quickly set out to hire someone who could do that for him. The next day he had set up three interviews. The first guy was great.
He knew everything he needed to and was very interesting. At the end of the interview Bob asked him, "Do you notice anything different about me?" The chap answered, "Why yes, I couldn't help but notice you've got no ears." Bob got very angry and threw him out. The second interview was with a woman, and she was even better than the first guy. He asked her the same question, "Do you notice anything different about me?" She replied, "Well, you've got no ears." Bob again was upset and threw her out. The third and last interview was the best of all three. It was with a very young woman who was fresh out of college.
Bob was anxious, but went ahead and asked the young woman the same question.
"Do you notice anything different about me?" To his surprise, the young woman answered,
"Yes. You wear contact lenses."
Bob was shocked, and said, "What an incredibly observant young woman. How in the world did you know that?"
The young woman replied,
"Well, it's pretty hard to wear glasses when you've got no ears!"

Where did the butcher dance?
At the meatball!

What do you call a bald teddy?
Fred bear!

How does a banana answer the phone?
Yellow?

What do you call a vampire's dog?
A werewoof!

What do you get if you cross a toadstool and a full suitcase?
Not mushroom for your clothes!

When does a cart come before a horse?
In the dictionary!

What weighs a ton and scares theatre audiences?
The Fat Tum of the Opera!

A young boy, about eight years old, was at the corner grocer's picking out a big box of washing powder. The grocer walked over and, trying to be friendly, asked the boy if he had a lot of clothes to do. "Oh, no clothes," the boy said, "I'm going to wash my dog." "But you shouldn't use this to wash your dog. It's very powerful and if you wash your dog in this he'll get sick. In fact, it might even kill him!" But the boy was not to be stopped and carried the washing powder to the counter, paid for it and left. About a week later the boy was back in the grocer's shop to buy some sweets. The grocer asked the boy how his dog was doing. "Oh, he died," the boy said. The grocer said he was sorry the dog died but added, "I tried to tell you not to use that powder on your dog." "Well," the boy replied, "I don't think it was the detergent that killed him." "Oh? What was it then?" said the grocer.
"I think it was the spin drier."

What happened to the man who couldn't tell putty from toothpaste?
His windows fell out!

A woman walked into the sitting room to find her husband stalking around with a fly swatter. "What are you doing?" she asked. "Hunting flies," he said. "Oh, did you get any?" she asked. "Yep, three male ones and two female ones," he replied. Intrigued, she asked, "How can you tell?"
He answered, "Three were on a beer can, two were on the phone!"

A man went to see a theatrical agent and told her he was the world's greatest bird impressionist.
"Bird Impressions are rubbish. Old hat. Yesterday's news. Not interested." she said.
"Suit yourself," said the man, and he flew out of the window.

What do you get if you cross an owl with a skunk?
A bird that smells but doesn't give a hoot!

What's wrapped in cling-film and rings bells?
The lunchpack of Notre Dame!

What is David Ginola's favourite ice cream flavour?
Aston Vanilla!

What goes up a drainpipe down, but not down one up?
An umbrella!

How does Luke Skywalker wish you a good day in springtime?
May the Fourth be with you!

The proud owner of an impressive new clock was showing it off to a friend. "This clock," he said, "will go for 14 days without winding."
"Really," replied his friend,
"and how long will it go if you do wind it?

Donald: Sorry I'm late, sir. My canary died of flu.
Teacher: Oh, I'm sorry, Donald. I didn't know canaries could die of flu...
Donald: Mine did, it flew into a bus!

What goes "Oh, Oh, Oh"?
Santa walking backwards!

What has green hair and runs through the forest?
Mouldy locks!

What's round and bad-tempered?
A vicious circle!

If all your clothes were stolen, what would you go home in?
The dark!

How does a witch tell the time?
With a witchwatch!

What do you call a very popular perfume?
A best-smeller!

Jack: You have the face of a saint.
Jill: Really? Which one?
Jack: Saint Bernard!

A young man had asked his girlfriend to marry him, and was formally asking her father for his permission.
"Sir," he said, "I would like to have your daughter for my wife."
"Why, can't she get one of her own?" said the father.

Patient: Doctor, it's my wife. She thinks she's a duck!
Doc: Good Lord! You had better bring her in to see me straight away.
Patient: I can't do that - she's flown south for the winter!

What kind of monster has the best hearing?
The eeriest!

Two Eskimos sitting in a kayak were chilly, but when they lit a fire in the craft it sank - proving once and for all that you can't have your kayak and heat it...

How can you drop an egg six feet without breaking it?
By dropping it seven feet - it won't break for the first six!

What happens if you play table tennis with a bad egg?
First it goes ping, then it goes pong!

Patient: Doctor, I can't help pulling ugly faces.
Doctor: Well there's nothing so terrible about that.
Patient: It is, the people with ugly faces don't like them being pulled!

What would you see at a chicken show?
Hentertainment!

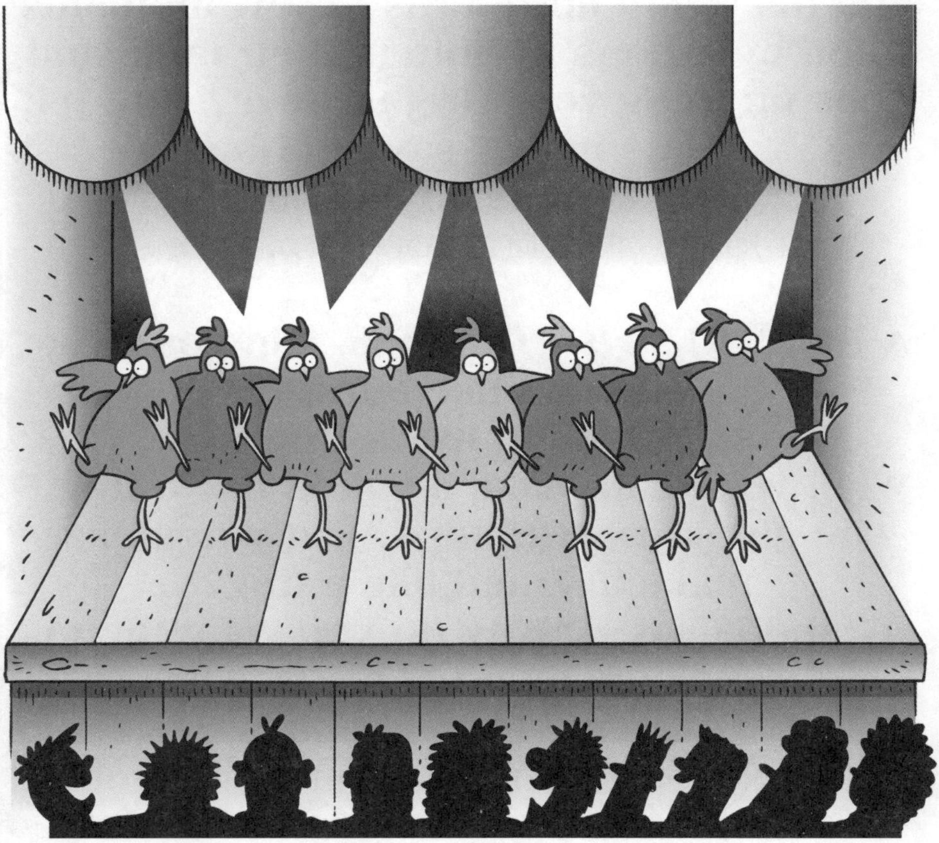

A young man was in a pub one day with his new girlfriend. It's their first date and everything is going well, apart from the odd silences. The girlfriend goes to the loo and while she is away, the young man spots somebody in the other bar that looks incredibly like Robbie Williams. He goes over for a look... "Excuse me," says the young man, "but you don't half look like Robbie Wiliams. I don't suppose....."
"Well," interrupts Rob, "actually I am Robbie Williams."
Well, the young man is almost speechless, but carries on,
"Look Robbie, I think you're brilliant. I've got all your records, I wonder if you could you do me a favour?"
"Whatever you want, mate," says Robbie.
"Well, you see, I'm in the other bar with my new girlfriend and it would really impress her if you would just come up to me and say 'Alright Steve?'"
"Sure, no problem," says Robbie.
So Steve rushes back into the other bar and his girlfriend returns. A few moments later, over pops Robbie to their table and goes up to Steve. "Alright Steve? How's it going mate?" says Robbie.
Steve looks up and says,
"Get lost Rob, can't you see I'm busy?"

A little girl says, "Grandpa, can you make a sound like a frog?"
"A sound like a frog?
Well, yes I can make a sound like a frog."
The girl says, "Grandpa, will you please make a sound like a frog?"
Grandpa says, "Why do you want me to make a sound like a frog?"
And the little girl says,
"Because Mummy said that when you croak, we're all going to Disneyland!"

A chemistry teacher wanted to teach his class a lesson about the evils of drinking, so he did an experiment with a glass of water, a glass of whisky and two worms. "Now, class. Watch the worms," said the teacher, putting one in the water. The worm jumped about, happy as could be. The second worm, he put into the whisky. It twitched painfully and quickly sank to the bottom, dead as a doornail. "Now, what lesson can we learn from this experiment?" the teacher asked. A boy raised his hand and said,
"Drink whisky and you won't get worms?"

What does Darth Maul shave with?
A laser blade!

A woman just back from Arizona was telling her friends about the trip. "When my husband first saw the Grand Canyon, his face dropped a mile," she said. "Why, was he disappointed with the view?"
"No, he fell over the edge."

One night during a violent thunderstorm a mother was tucking her small boy into bed. She was about to turn off the light when he asked with a wobble in his voice, "Mummy, can you sleep in my room tonight?" The mother smiled and gave him a reassuring hug. "I can't, sweetie," she said, "I have to sleep in Daddy's room." A long silence was broken by his little voice:
"The big sissy."

What is the difference between ammonia and pneumonia?
Ammonia comes in bottles, pneumonia comes in chests!

A little boy went up to his father one day and asked him:
"Dad, where did all of my intelligence come from, you or Mum?"
His father replied:
"Well, son, you must have got it from your mother, I still have mine."

Johnny was eating breakfast one morning and got to thinking about things.
"Mummy, why does daddy have so few hairs on his head?" he asked his mum.
"He thinks a lot," replied his mother, pleased with herself for coming up with a good answer.
Johnny thought for a second and said,
"I'm glad you don't do any thinking. You'd look silly bald!"

Bert went to visit his local vet.
"Doctor," he said sadly, "I'm afraid I'm going to have to ask you to cut off my dog's tail."
The vet stepped back, shocked.
"Bert, why would I want to do such a terrible thing?"
"Well, my mother-in-law's arriving tomorrow, and I don't want anything to make her think she's welcome."

After his annual physical examination, an elderly patient asked his doctor,
"Tell me, how long am I going to live?"
"Don't worry," his doctor replied,
"you'll probably live to be 84."
"But Doctor, I am 84!" he said.
"See? I told you!"

What do Paddington, Rupert and Pooh pack when they go on holiday?
Just the bear essentials!

What do you call a multi-storey pig pen?
A sty scraper!

Two hikers are in the woods and they come across a huge hole in the ground. One of them says, "Hey, let's throw something down there and see how deep it is." So they find a stone the size of a tennis ball and throw it down the hole expecting to hear a noise. But none came. So they look for something larger and find a rock the size of a basketball and throw it down the hole. They still hear no noise. So they walk along a path to look for something big enough to make a noise, and they come across a motorbike. They return to the hole and throw it down. A couple of seconds go by and they still hear nothing. Suddenly a goat comes charging straight at them and jumps right into the hole without even seeming to think about it. The men are amazed at what they've just seen. Then a farmer comes walking by. He stops and looks at the two hikers. "Have you seen my goat? I had him about 100 yards from here," he says. The hikers tell the man they have just seen a goat jump straight into the big hole. The farmer stares at them and says,
"No, that can't have been mine. My goat was tethered to a motorbike"

What do you get if you cover your garden with sugar?
Ants in your plants!

What's red and white on the outside, and grey on the inside?
Campbell's cream of elephant soup!

What did the fat man prove when he was run over by a steamroller?
That he had a lot of guts!

What do you get if you cross an electric eel and a sponge?
Shock absorbers!

What happened to the man who put his false teeth in backwards?
He ate himself!

What kind of car does Mickey Mouse's wife drive?
A minnie van!

An Italian, a Scotsman, and a Chinese man are hired at a construction site. The foreman points out a huge pile of sand and tells the Italian guy that he is in charge of sweeping. He tells the Scotsman that he is in charge of the shovelling. The Chinese guy is in charge of supplies. The foreman goes away for a couple of hours and when he returns, the pile of sand is still there untouched. He asks the Italian guy, "Why haven't you swept any of this sand?" The Italian guy says, "I no hava da broom. You saida da Chinese fella was in charge a da supplies, but he hasa disappeared and I no coulda finda him nowhere!" The foreman then turns to the Scotsman and says, "You were supposed to shovel this pile of sand." The Scotsman says, "Aye, but ah could'ne get masel' a shoovel. Ye left th' Chinese laddie in charge of supplies, but ah could'ne find him either, Boss." The foreman is really angry and storms off toward the pile of sand. He is looking for the Chinese guy.
Just then, the Chinese guy leaps out from behind the the pile of sand and shouts, "SUPPLIES!"

From a cruise ship, everyone on board can see a bearded man on a small island, desperately shouting and waving his arms about frantically. "Who is that?" a passenger asks the captain. "I've no idea," says the captain, "but every year when we pass this island, he goes mental!"

An old man was eating in a motorway café when three Hell's Angels bikers walked in. The first walked up to the old man, pushed his cigarette into the old man's pie and then took a seat at the counter. The second walked up to the old man and knocked over his glass of milk before taking a seat at the counter. The third walked up to the old man, turned over the old man's plate and then took a seat at the counter. Without a word of protest, the old man quietly left the café. One of the bikers said to the waitress, "Hmph, not much of a man, was he?" The waitress replied, "He's not much of a lorry driver either. He just backed his truck over three motorbikes."

A guy goes to his doctor and says: "Doctor, my wife and I have a real problem. We're tired all the time." The doctor says: "I think the problem is lack of exercise. I suggest that you start walking seven miles every day. Call me in a week and let me know how you get on." A week later the man phones the doctor and tells him he feels much better. The doctor asks: "Well how's your wife?" The man replies: "How should I know, I'm 49 miles away."

A Swiss man, looking for directions, pulls up at a bus stop where two English blokes are waiting.
"Entschuldigung, können Sie Deutsch sprechen?" he says.
The two Englishmen just stare at him.
"Excusez-moi, parlez-vous Français?"
The two continue to stare.
"Parlare Italiano?" No response.
"¿Hablan ustedes Español?" Still nothing.
The Swiss guy drives off, obviously disgusted.
The first English bloke turns to the second and says, "You know, maybe we should learn a foreign language."
"What for?" says the other, "that bloke knew four languages, and it didn't do him any good!"

Why did the tap dancer retire?
He kept falling in the sink!

Movie Madness!

Some new projects from Hollywood...

Flood! starring Wendy Raincomes
Shark Attack starring Arthur Legleft
Mars Invades starring Des Analien
Lost in the City by Ron Tern
I'm a Duck! starring Don B Silly
The Werewolf starring Harry Face
Volcano Eruption starring Luke D Topblue
Rogue Elephant starring Ida Flathead
Deadline starring Dustin Time
Shotgun Wedding starring Marion Haste
The Picnickers starring Tina K. Kortoo
Frankenstein's Mistake starring Ed Felloff
Raindrops from Heaven starring Ruth Leeks
What's Your Story? starring Alec Splane
Money to Burn starring Ritchie Nuff
The Bank Job starring Phil D Baggup
Ten Seconds to Impact starring Willy Maykit
Feel Aladdin's Anger starring Nick Hislamp

One of the best marksmen in the Metropolitan Police was passing through a small village. Everywhere he saw evidence of the most incredible shooting. On trees, on walls, and on fences there were numerous little bull's-eyes painted with a bullet hole right in the middle. The policeman asked one of the villagers if he could meet the person responsible for this wonderful shooting. The person turned out to be the village idiot.
"This is the best marksmanship I have ever seen!" said the policeman, "How in the world do you do it?"
"It's easy," said the idiot, "I shoot first and draw the circles afterwards."

What is hairy and coughs?
A coconut with a cold!

A man is shopping in the local supermarket. He selects some milk, some eggs, a carton of juice, and a pack of bacon. As he unloads his items at the checkout to pay, a girl standing behind him in line watches him put the four items on the belt and says: "You must be single." The man looks at the four items on the belt, and seeing nothing unusual about them says, "That's right. How on Earth did you know?"
She replies, "Because you're really ugly."

The doctor took Dan into the room and said, "Dan, I have some good news and some bad news."
Dan said, "Give me the good news."
"They're going to name a disease after you."

A lorry driver was driving along the road. He passed a sign that said "LOW BRIDGE AHEAD." But it was too late, he got stuck under the bridge, and cars were backed up for miles behind him. Finally, a police car pulled up. The policeman got out of his car and walked around to the lorry driver, put his hands on his hips and said, "Oh dear, oh dear. Got stuck, did you?"
The truck driver said,
"No officer, I was just delivering this bridge and I've run out of petrol"

An angry motorist went back to a garage where he'd purchased an expensive battery for his car six months earlier. "Listen," the motorist grumbled to the owner of the garage, "when I bought that battery you said it would be the last battery my car would ever need. It died after only six months!"
"Sorry," said the garage owner, "I didn't think your car would last that long."

Why can't a leopard hide?
Because he's always spotted!

What do you get if you cross a penguin and an elk?
A chocolate moose!

A man is in bed with his wife when he hears a knock on the front door. He rolls over, looks at the clock and sees that it's three o'clock in the morning. "What idiot would be knocking at the door at this hour?" thinks the man, and he rolls over and tries to go back to sleep.
After a few minutes, there's a louder knock on the door.
"Aren't you going to see who it is?" asks his wife. So the man drags himself out of bed and goes downstairs. He opens the door to find a stranger standing outside.
"Hey, mate," says the stranger, "can you give us a push?" "No! Get lost! It's three in the morning. I was asleep!" says the man. He goes back to bed and tells his wife what happened. She says,
"Remember that night when we broke down in the pouring rain and you had to knock on that man's door to get him to help us? What would have happened if he'd told us to get lost?"
So the man gets out of bed again, gets dressed and goes downstairs. He opens the door and, not being able to see the stranger anywhere, he shouts, "Hey. Do you still want a push?" A voice cries out, "Yes, please." So, still being unable to see the stranger, the man shouts, "Where are you?"
"I'm over here on the swings."

What flag do you salute in the jungle?
The Tarzan stripes!

Mail

If you enjoyed this book, you can find more hilarious jokes, amazing facts, and brainbusting riddles and puzzles in the following books, also published by Dean:

Title	ISBN
The World's Funniest Animal Jokes for Kids	0 603 56064 4
The World's Funniest Disgusting Jokes for Kids	0 603 56065 2
The World's Funniest School Jokes for Kids	0 603 56063 6
The World's Most Amazing Animal Facts for Kids	0 603 56060 1
The World's Most Amazing Planet Earth Facts for Kids	0 603 56062 8
The World's Most Amazing Science Facts for Kids	0 603 56061X
1000 of the World's Most Astonishing Facts for Kids	0 603 56067 9
1000 of the World's Greatest Brainbusters	0 603 56068 7